Selling on the Phone

Selling on the Phone

A Self-Teaching Guide

James D. Porterfield

THE WILEY PRESS
John Wiley & Sons, Inc.
New York • Chichester • Brisbane • Toronto • Singapore

This book is dedicated
to my father,
Orville L. Porterfield,
in appreciation for his
faith in me

PERMISSIONS ACKNOWLEDGMENTS

pp. 105–106. Adapted from *Becoming a Writer*, by Dorothea Brande. Copyright © 1934 by Harcourt, Brace & Company. Copyright © 1961 by Gilbert I. Coolins and Justin Brande. Foreword © 1981 by J.P. Tarcher, Inc. Reprinted by J.P Tarcher, Inc., and Houghton Mifflin Company.

p. 107. Adapted from *Telemarketing: High-Profit Telephone Selling Techniques*, by Gerald J. Ortland. Copyright © 1982 by John Wiley & Sons, Inc., New York.

pp. 115–116. From *Power Selling by Telephone*, by Barry Z. Masser and William M. Leeds. Copyright © 1982 by Parker Publishing Company, Inc. Published by Parker Publishing Company, Inc., West Nyack, NY.

Library of Congress Cataloging in Publication Data
Porterfield, James D.
Selling On The Phone.
  (A Self-teaching guide)
  Includes index.
  1. Telephone selling. I. Title. II. Series.
HF5438.3.P67 1985   658.8′5   84-17403
ISBN 0-471-88450-2

Printed in the United States of America

10 9 8 7 6 5 4 3 2

Acknowledgments

I would like to extend thanks to several people instrumental in enabling me to learn and apply the material presented. First to Robert Farkas, who helped me go from failure to success in selling. And to John Ferraro, owner of Corporate Management Systems, Inc., who enabled me to convert what I know into successful seminars. To Ruth Cavin, the Developmental Editor at John Wiley & Sons, who turned the manuscript around with speed, patience, and understanding. To others at John Wiley & Sons, especially Judy Wilson, John Ware, and Betsy Perry—my editor, who got the project moving to completion. And finally, to the following reviewers, whose valuable input resulted in a vastly improved book: Mary Ann Kroop, Franklin Kavaler, Allen Simeone, E. Jack Pudney, Gail Cohen, Tom Stanton, Harold Brown, Al Pratico, Diane Loucks, Eileen Hauptman, Martha Trexler, Virginia McNeill, Mark J. Heller, Regina Quartararo, and Bernard Cohen.

Contents

Before You Begin

This book was written primarily for two distinct groups of readers: individual tellesellers beginning work in a large marketing organization, and sales representatives or other business people who want to use the telephone to increase their productivity. As a result, occasionally information is presented that may be applicable only to one group or the other. In addition, there is occasional discussion of management decisions beyond the authority of a selling staff. But since these decisions can affect the work of either group, and since many progressive marketing organizations welcome suggestions for improved operations from the staff, I have chosen to include these in the text. I believe that all members of a sales team can benefit from a full understanding of the total telemarketing operation, from overall management concerns to daily teleselling sessions.

For you to get full value for the time you spend using this book, you should keep certain of my opinions and beliefs in mind:

1. *Selling is an art, not a science.* For this reason, you *won't* find such magic formulas as "the 7 keys to an effective opening," "the 8 secrets of closing a sale," or "14 steps to making a million dollars in sales in 3 weeks." You *will* find suggestions, outlines, and forms to help you develop a natural teleselling style that is based on your own strengths and abilities. Upon completion of the book you will have developed the basic skills needed to be the unique teleseller only you can be, and to be successful at your work.

2. *You learn by doing, not by reading how others do.* As a sales manager, sales trainer, and seminar instructor, I adhered to this principle, and with excellent results. You will see the philosophy reflected here in several ways:

   a. As a well-motivated, mature professional, working (perhaps out of necessity) with an eye to both job and financial satisfaction, you want to do the best you can. Your motivation and drive will enable you to learn by doing yourself (the reason self-teaching guides exist) rather than by being hand-led through one person's way of working.

   b. There are no teleselling scripts or contrived sales dialogues in the body of this book. Instead, suggested sales phraseology is provided throughout, to start you thinking about what you want to say in the situations you encounter. But ultimately it will fall on you to develop your scripts or outlines for extemporaneous calls, try them out, and revise them as needed to make them work for you. That is how it will be in your work; this book merely starts you in that direction.

c. The Interlude: A Special Activity on page 33 is intended to begin this self-teaching process for you. While it may appear contradictory to urge you throughout to plan your calls and what you are going to say once you are on the telephone, yet tell you to get on the telephone for a day before you begin the skill-building sections of the book, I believe the benefit to you of completing the Interlude outweighs the example it sets. The activity will set in your mind, more than any urging, why the remainder of the book is important.

3. *Keep it simple.* Woody Hayes, legendary football coach at Ohio State University, taught his players that "if you get fancy, you get beat." Keep your goals simple and attainable. Keep your product choices for the prospect simple. Keep your selling message simple. To the extent you are able to do this, you will win the undying gratitude, not to mention the business, of your customers and prospects.

One final note: The telephone can be used to sell all manner of products and services, from encyclopedias to office decoration and maintenance services. For the sake of word economy, though, I refer throughout the book to products only. When you read "product," you can substitute "service" without changing the application or meaning.

How to Use This Book

Selling on the Phone is designed to be a complete basic course in selling by telephone. To gain maximum benefit from your work with it, the following procedures will prove helpful:

1. Read the Table of Contents. It outlines the chapters and gives you a brief introduction to all the skills needed to be successful as a tele-seller.
2. Leaf through the book, reading the Keys that are boxed at the head of each chapter. Taken together, these give you a minicourse in the basics of teleselling, and set up for you an overview of the teleselling process and your role in it.
3. Read the Introduction and complete the "Preliminary Skills and Atti-tude Survey," including the goal-setting portion.
4. Go to Chapter 1 and complete it and each succeeding chapter in order. You are strongly urged to complete all activities within each chapter as you come to them.
5. At the conclusion of each chapter, complete the Self-Inventory, as-sess your strengths and weaknesses, and check your understanding of the chapter by answering the questions before going on to the next chapter.
6. Begin working on the telephone as soon as possible, no later than at the completion of Section II. The Interlude gets you started. Apply the "learn by doing" principle, letting both the book and your experience be your teacher. The world is full of prospects, more than you will ever be able to contact. And most are forgiving, should you have to recon-tact them later, when you are more effective.
7. After you have completed the book and the concluding questionnaire, come back to it occasionally and redo both the Self-Inventories and concluding test. Compare your new scores with your old ones to measure your improved skills and attitudes toward your work.
8. Begin a lifelong professional reading program, as recommended in the Afterword. The bibliography can provide a starting point, and sugges-tions as to how you can keep up your reading program are presented at several locations in the book.

Introduction

You have elected to use an exciting and challenging selling medium: the telephone. The use of the telephone as a way of selling is a relatively new phenomenon, and your decision to join this movement means that you will have to learn a number of new skills. But a reminder before you start: Using the telephone only changes one aspect of your selling work, the *method* of delivering your sales message. The selling process and the basic skills needed to sell have not been changed, although the emphasis on certain skills has been shifted.

In order for you to succeed at teleselling, three things will be required of you. First, you must be well versed in basic selling skills, the techniques you employ day in and day out while doing your job. Second, you must know your products inside out. And finally you must communicate what you know in a manner that gets sales. This book has been written to help you equip yourself with the needed techniques and skills to be a successful teleseller professional.

If you are an experienced salesperson but beginning to sell by telephone for the first time, you will still benefit from following this book from start to finish. The transition from outside sales to teleselling will require some adaptation on your part. The skills and abilities needed in both are the same, but certain skills take on increased importance in telephone selling. For example, the words you use not only have to tell your story but, because you are not in the presence of the prospect, must also fully describe the product and its benefits and enable the prospect to envision using it. Other sales techniques, such as product demonstrations or group selling, are less important or completely inapplicable.

These are but a few of the differences between teleselling and face-to-face selling. Other factors are unique to telephone work:

1. You generally have a shorter time to conduct your sales call.
2. You cannot, without prior planning, contact, and work, use printed sales aids. You'd have to mail them in advance or deliver them later.
3. Your audience is often national, but with local problems and prejudices of their own, which you must be prepared to deal with.
4. It takes hard work to establish trust and empathy with only a voice—that is, without benefit of a smile and a handshake.

Throughout the book you will be given a chance to evaluate yourself and your performance, set goals, and learn techniques to improve your work habits so you can meet those goals. To begin, here is a survey of your present skills and attitudes. Another, at the end of the book, is an evaluation of your telephone sales skills. The Self-Inventories throughout the book are designed to help you evaluate where you are, so you can get where you want to be. By taking the time to complete them, you will be able to identify your strengths and weaknesses. If you cannot confidently answer "Yes" to all the questions, you will then know where to concentrate your efforts at improving your skill and success. You will learn what goals to set for yourself. You will know what follow-up activities to undertake for future improvement.

Now turn to page 1 and begin to sell successfully on the telephone.

Selling on the Phone

Preliminary Skills and Attitudes Survey

Answer the questions below, feeling free, where appropriate, to comment beyond "yes" and "no." After completing the fourteen questions, review your answers and set at least three goals for yourself as you work through the chapters that follow. These should reflect your motives for picking up this book in the first place.

1. Do I have a call plan before I get on the telephone?

    _____
    _____

2. Do I handle my calls in a manner that inspires confidence in me and the way my company is managed?

    _____
    _____

3. Do I gain and keep my prospect's attention throughout the call?

    _____
    _____

4. Do I always deliver a well-thought-out, logical selling message?

    _____
    _____

5. Do my prospects hear and comprehend what I say to them?

    _____
    _____

6. Do I have a selling strategy I employ in each telephone call I handle?

    _____
    _____

7. What techniques do I use to determine a prospect's wants or needs?

    _____
    _____

8. Am I attentive to what my prospect says, or do I have to ask that things be repeated?

    _____
    _____

9. Do my prospects understand me, or do I find occasionally that I have to explain what I mean?

    _____
    _____

10. Can I distinguish between a product's characterstics or features, the resulting advantages, and how a prospect benefits from them? Which do I sell?

_____

_____

11. What major objections to buying do I encounter?

_____

_____

12. How, and how well, do I handle these objections?

_____

_____

13. Do I handle rejection well enough so that it doesn't discourage me?

_____

_____

14. What obstacles do I encounter that interfere with my ability to communicate effectively with my prospects?

_____

_____

15. My goals for completing this book are:

_____

_____

CHAPTER 1

An Introduction to Telemarketing

The Key

> The telephone is coming into increasing use as a way of bringing salespeople into contact with their prospective and existing customers. Regardless of the purpose of the contact—"cold" calling to find prospects, qualifying those prospects, making appointments, closing sales, or servicing customers—the telephone can be used to conduct all the business an outside salesperson does. This chapter discusses the many benefits of telephone selling, enabling you to consider its applications to your work.

The technology that makes a book like this one useful to a large number of people was put into service less than fifteen years ago. And it is only in the last five years that a number of other factors have made telephone selling an attractive alternative to the more established sales channels. But today the telephone has changed forever the way things are sold.

Reasons to Use the Telephone in Selling

The first call using a WATS line was made in 1968. This may not be ranked by popular historians with Alexander Graham Bell's "Mr. Watson, come here. I want you!" But what was said is dwarfed in importance by the enormous ramifications of the event. Outbound WATS, or Wide Area Telephone Service, enables the placing of long-distance calls at a fixed rate, rather than at the more expensive per-call cost. Combined with inbound WATS, or 800 service, low-cost and large-scale use of the telephone by businesses, even over large geographic areas, has become a reality.

Today technology that allows easy, inexpensive, and fast access to virtually all markets is at hand. There is the sophisticated device known as the electronic dialer, which automatically goes through a call list, playing a prerecorded message to the answering party. The message can be worded to appeal only to qualified prospects, who then either stay on the line to speak with a human teleseller, or leave the acknowledgment that will initiate a call back.

For larger telemarketing operations, there is call-routing equipment. This automatically route a call through the various long-distance services the user subscribes to, such as AT&T Long Lines, SDS, Sprint or MCI, and places it on the least-expensive line available at that moment.

The rapidly expanding market for this equipment and these services, which lower costs and improve productivity, along with the competition among supplying companies to meet demand, has made sophisticated technology available to even the smallest user of telemarketing. It has been estimated that the annual volume of telephone use now exceeds 200 billion calls, at an annual cost in excess of $9 billion.

The use of the telephone as a marketing tool was also inevitable because of its omnipresence in our lives. Anyone can pick up a telephone handset and call into 97.5 percent of the homes in America and virtually 100 percent of the businesses, generally within a matter of seconds. As a marketer, whether to consumers or to other businesses, you can certainly go more places on a one-to-one basis more quickly and easily by telephone than via any other medium.

Another factor that has made the telephone so important as a marketing tool has been the high cost of all other direct-selling methods. While estimates of the actual cost of a single outside sales visit made by a representative vary widely, the significant finding is that the cost per call has increased by as much as 49 percent in the past five years, to estimated amounts in excess of $200. Ways must be found to reduce the cost of a sales contact. Equally important, if sales contacts are to be made in person, they can be cost effective only if they are made to prospects who are highly likely to buy.

If you are selling outside at present, you can determine your own cost of sales using the table on page 5. Refer to your expense records and experience so the numbers will be as accurate as possible. If you are already a teleseller working for a company that has outside salespeople and you want to compare your performance to theirs, this data may be available from them or from sales management.

After completing the table, determine how many sales you (or the typical company field-sales representative) made in the past year. Divide that number into the total dollars spent. You now have a simple estimate of the cost of the sales provided by field work.

Direct-mail marketing has also experienced cost increases. The Direct Mail Marketing Association reports that the cost of a relatively simple direct-mail package aimed at 250,000 prospects has increased as much as 46 percent since 1976. And despite increasingly sophisticated mailing-list management and selection techniques, there has been little improvement in the overall 1 to 2 percent response rate. At today's prices, the cost per thousand for a typical large mailing (100,000 pieces) can be between $300 and $400 per thousand. That makes the cost of a sale, with a 1 percent response rate, $30 to $40. And not all products lend themselves to direct-mail selling exclusively.

Selling by telephone can be expensive, too. In addition to salaries, rent, furniture, supplies, and other expenses associated with operating an office, there is the cost of acquiring telephone directories or mailing lists that include telephone numbers, and, of course, the special equipment and long-distance services required. But even so, experience has shown that, at the rate of

Field Sales Staff Expenses

Item	Past Year	This Year
Automobile Purchase		
Automobile Operation		
Fuel		
Tolls/Fares		
Parking		
Maintenance		
Taxis		
Air/Rail Travel		
Lodging		
Entertainment		
Salary		
Totals		
Comments:		

1 sale in 10 completed calls to those you suspect may buy, even moderate-sized telemarketing operations can realize a cost of sale of only $15 to $25. *Sales & Marketing Management* reported in 1981 that Inter-Continental Hotels had documented the cost of each telephone call at $10, at a time when field-staff calls were averaging $80.

Today companies are facing increasingly stiff competition for consumer dollars. Widening product options and more numerous suppliers invite the shopper to search out the best choice. Marketers are finding it necessary to work smarter, making the most of the finite number of hours available to get their message out and close business. Use of the telephone offers time savings for both parties to a sale, the prospect and the teleseller. Many buyers will tell you they prefer dealing with the time-sensitive salesperson who makes some or all sales contact by telephone. It is being increasingly accepted that business-to-business telephone marketing is more effective than face-to-face selling. Consumer marketers, especially catalog marketers and media advertisers using 800 service, also report unprecedented results.

The telephone is a uniquely versatile marketing tool. It puts, literally at your fingertips, the flexibility to respond to changing needs, new situations or product/market mixes, without an elaborate retooling of your marketing methods. For example, envision the impact of a significant new pricing strategy on a sales staff. If they are outside, first each salesperson would have to be notified, whether by mail, telephone, or a summons to the home office. Then a lot of time would be expended as the representatives traveled among their customers and prospects to explain the pricing policy, trying to close additional business.

By contrast, the fact that all telesellers work from the same location makes getting information to the sales staff a simple matter of calling a morning meeting. The time it takes for the new policy to affect sales is cut down, too, as tellsellers go to work on the telephone to contact their customers and/or prospects almost immediately. An entire new policy could be explained and taken advantage of in as little as one day.

As a telemarketing operation grows, an additional benefit will be realized: easier, more efficient, and closer supervision of the selling operation.

To help in deciding what your purpose will be in using telemarketing in your company or work, follow the suggestions below:

1. List the factors outlined here that prompted you to investigate telemarketing as an alternative to your present sales and marketing activity.
2. Which of the telephone's strengths do you expect to benefit from? As specifically as possible, comment on how you plan to benefit from each strength you have listed.

What Is Telemarketing?

Joan Eisner of Performance Achievement Group, a firm that specializes in telemarketing, sees telemarketing as an important direct-response tool, perhaps the largest advertising medium in the United States today. Rudy Oetting of R. H. Oetting and Associates, in the Direct Marketing Association/Telemarketing Council's publication *Telephone Marketing,* had defined telemarketing as "a direct marketing medium through which products or services can be offered or discussed when a combination of *systematic activities* and *telecommunications devices* brings a *trained and prepared human being* into a *tightly controlled dialogue* with another human being who has been *carefully selected* for contact based on characteristics [that] indicate close affinity with those products and services." (Italics mine.)

The important thing for you to note in Oetting's definition is that, with one exception, the elements apply to *all* marketing techniques. All of selling is a combination of *systematic activities* carried out by *trained people,* conducted in a *controlled* environment with prospects who have been *carefully selected.* The unique element is the medium, the *telecommunications device.*

There are other factors common to all marketing plans and activities. They are worth noting as you begin to plan greater use of the telephone in sales. They include:

1. *The establishment of objectives.* Your objectives can be expressed as a gross or net sales dollar target, or as a percent of market share. Or they can be measurable activities that you know will lead to sales, such as soliciting leads, qualifying prospects, or setting up appointments. Regardless of what your goals are, be sure they are measurable and realistic.
2. *The establishment and maintenance of control over your activity.* Controls will enable you to determine whether you meet the goals you set. If you see you are falling short, you can then evaluate what adjustments to make.

3. *Allocation of the necessary resources to achieve the goals.* This includes both financial and human resources.
4. *A known and planned-for sales call flow and product-presentation strategy*—a prescribed or recommended way to get from prospecting to closing. This should include an interview opener, questions to ask, a list of objections that are likely to occur and how to answer them, a plan for when to ask for the order, and a decision as to how big the order should be to be worth the time needed to close it.
5. *Careful screening to ensure that you are calling on the right prospects.* Before you pick up the telephone, you will know whom you are calling and why.
6. *A product that you know to be of use and value to its intended market.* You cannot expect to get very far if even you do not believe in your product.

What the Telephone Can Do for You

Once you understand clearly what you can achieve with the telephone, you can go on to the important decision of where to use it. This decision can and will vary from company to company, from telemarketing campaign to telemarketing campaign, and from market to market.

First, determine your needs, goals, and wishes. Do you plan to use the telephone only for a segment of your selling activity, or will you rely on telemarketing for the entire sales process? Whichever you decide, you should then tailor your application of the telephone to the decision.

Among the many applications available to you, the first is the ability to generate leads. In the broadest sense, a lead is anyone among your target audience (those you suspect could become customers) who you know has a need for your product. Whether your leads are collected from your usual source, by electronic dialing, or by a different telemarketing department or organization, you can use the telephone to qualify them further to make sure the person not only needs your product, but will buy now or in the near future, has the available money to buy, and has the authority to make a buying decision.

Even if you produce qualified leads (prospects) in some other way than by telephone, the telephone will allow you to follow them up quickly and efficiently for sales action. It is always good practice for you to always leave the door open to a follow-up call, and there are several ways to do this: You may call to inquire if the information you sent recently has arrived, or to present additional, "new" information of interest to the prospect. If your selling cycle is a long one, this may be a planned technique to keep the prospect's interest in your product high.

If you are managing field salespeople and using the telephone to support them, you can reduce your average cost per call by helping a field representative make more calls that produce results and fewer that don't. You always want your outside salespeople to spend their time on high-priority prospects who are ready to make a buying decision. Working from a list of leads who have been qualified in some way (those who responded to ads, direct mail, former or present customers, and so on), an initial interview can be conducted by telephone, preparing the prospect for a sales call, and setting up an appointment. The telephone can also be used to gather the information needed to make the salesperson's visit the most effective possible. And the telephone can often be used to contact parties who can influence the buying decision but who are hard or inappropriate to see.

With someone else providing that telephone support, the outside salesperson is free to spend 100 percent of his or her time in face-to-face selling with ready-to-buy prospects. You have eliminated the need for the sales representative to spend days in the office trying to make appointments, or wasting time following unproductive leads. The most important factor in such a system is that the teleseller work cooperatively with the salesperson.

Telephone contact can be established after some other marketing campaign has been instituted. It is especially effective to combine teleselling with one or more additional marketing activities. A telephone call might follow a direct-mail piece, an advertisement, or a salesperson's visit. The goals for such calls can range from further qualifying prospects, to answering objections, to closing business, and it should be clear what those goals are. Is it reasonable to expect a one-call close (a sale completed in only one call) or will it take further contact? What form should further contact take? Once you have established the goal for your call, you can plan what you will say.

The telephone is especially effective as a means of keeping in touch with existing accounts. The value of keeping a hard-gained customer satisfied cannot be overestimated. You can call when your records indicate the customer's supply of your product or its accessories is running low. Or when you think, from your knowledge of your market and its buying cycle, a peak need for your product will exist. Similarly, you should review your inactive former accounts and reactivate any of those you can. Say you are calling simply because you want to "update your records"; you can then follow with a presentation of your new products or prices. In all cases, if you have a valid reason for calling, you will achieve results. The telephone lets you keep in touch with your customers, provide caring service, and learn of new developments that will enable you to keep your competitive edge, and it does all of this effectively, frequently and inexpensively. Of course, getting orders is the major goal of the teleseller.

To further help you plan your use of telemarketing, review this section and fill in the table on page 9.

Your telephone should not be thought of as a second choice in selling. In the 1980's, the telephone may become the primary method of selling. It emphatically is not a less-than-perfect substitute for having an outside representative call on customers. Telesellers can achieve all that outside representatives can for their customers and their company. They can establish a presence, build rapport, fill business needs, service, befriend, and create an identity and image for their company, their product and themselves.

In increasing numbers, sales and marketing executives are learning that it is no longer economically practical to market solely through an outside sales staff. With the inefficiences inherent in a system using outside sales represen-

Determining Where and How to Use the Telephone

Marketing activity	How presently handled	How tele-marketing can help	Set a goal	Follow-up activity
Produce prospects				
Qualify and control ad leads				
Make appointments				
Reactivate in-active accts.				
Sell low vol. accts./terr.				
Increase sales on in-bound calls				

SELF INVENTORY Yes No

1. I know which of my marketing activities will benefit most from telemarketing. ___ ___
2. I presently make use of the telephone to conduct some selling activity. ___ ___
3. My use of the telephone in sales is coordinated with other marketing methods. ___ ___
4. I find the telephone as useful and professional in selling as making face-to-face calls on a prospect or customer. ___ ___
5. I know what results I have to achieve to demonstrate the effectiveness of the telephone in my marketing strategy. ___ ___

tatives exclusively, trying to move prospects to a closed sale is very expensive. Whether you are integrating the telephone into one or more of the steps in the selling process that apply to your business, or plan to devote the entire process to the telephone, you and your company will experience cost reduction, increased efficiency, greater productivity, and, most important, greater profits.

For Thought and Action

How do you measure up on the performance goals of this chapter, as tested above?

Now that you've completed Chapter 1, how are you going to change your work?

Before going on to Chapter 2, have you decided what marketing activities you are going to conduct over the telephone?

CHAPTER 2

What Goes into a Sale

The Key

Your sales work on the telephone is critical to the success of your company. It is important for you to maintain high personal and professional standards in your contact with prospects and customers. To do this and be a successful teleseller, you should understand how your prospects react to your contact with them and why they react as they do. Of equal importance to you is why people buy what you are selling. If you understand these two things about each prospect—reaction and buying motivation—you will be able to tailor your call behavior to the prospect and close more sales. This chapter will let you determine what type of salesperson you are. You can then evaluate the things about you prospects react to, and also their major motivations to buy.

There are at least two participants in each sale: you, the teleseller, and the prospect-turned-customer, whether an individual consumer or the buyer for a business or other organization. In more complex decision-making situations, there may be more than one person on either or both ends of the sale. Even traditional individual sales, such as home improvements or delivery of services, can require discussion with two people, husband and wife. Complex business sales of such items as technical services or electronic equipment, which often affects more than one department, may require multiple contributors to the selling and buying decision on the part of both vendor and customer.

You and Selling

Do you realize how important you are when you are selling? Consider, for example, how much revenue you produce. Do you have a sales quota? If so, write the amount here: $_____. Or perhaps you know your volume, how many dollars worth of business you do (or should do) in a day, week, month, quarter, or year. If so, write that amount here: $_____ per _____. Whether you go by your goal or your record of productivity, you can see that you generate a substantial amount of money for your company.

Another way to look at your worth, and perhaps more important to you, is to consider the profits you can produce for your company in your selling activity. If you know or can find out your company's net profit as a percentage, write that percent here: _____%. (If the information is not available to you, use the overall percentage for American business in 1984: 4.8%.)

Go back to either your sales quota or your volume and write that number here: $_____. Multiply it by the profit percentage of your company or the 4.8 percent figure. This equals your profit potential to your company: $_____. You can create that profit *if* you meet your quota or maintain your productivity.

You can also consider your importance in terms of what it costs to have you at work. Begin by completing the following table (for one year):

Salary	$ _____
Travel	+ _____
Meals	+ _____
Lodging	+ _____
Entertainment	+ _____
Samples, etc.	+ _____
Overhead	+ _____
TOTAL	$ _____
Divided by 10 = $_____	
and × 4 (benefits)	+ _____
GRAND TOTAL	= $ _____

Now write, in total dollars, the amount of your average sale: $_____. Divide this amount into the grand total above. How many sales do you have to close just for your company to break even on your work? Looked at another way, the total number of sales you made, divided into the grand-total cost, tells you what one of your sales costs your company: $_____.

Like your company, your prospects and customers also put considerable trust in you. If you do your job well, you add to the quality of their work or personal lives. If you do your job poorly, or in some way manipulate a person into making a bad purchase, you not only damage your own and your company's reputations, you needlessly hurt your prospect or customer.

To meet your obligations to your company and to present and potential customers and be a successful teleseller, you must know your products inside and out, their characteristics and specifications and what benefits they will provide for the customer. You also have to be able to persuade people to buy the products you have to offer. To do this you'll need an action-getting telephone strategy that will serve you in all sales situations, up to the final point of asking for the order. This is true whether you are a teleseller, or an outside salesperson who just wants to use the telephone more effectively.

You must have the ability to communicate effectively with your prospects and customers. Certain communications skills assume prime importance in telephone selling: your voice, vocabulary, and listening ability are critical because they aren't supplemented by physical appearance, facial expression, and other visual elements. It is therefore necessary that you deliver your sales message in a clear, concise, methodical, and understandable manner, a manner that compensates for the absence of face-to-face interaction and the opportunity to demonstrate your product.

There are also certain attitudes you must develop in order to be successful. You will have to be tough if you are to drive yourself in the face of the inevitable rejections you will encounter. Because you will complete some 18 to 180 telephone calls a day, you will meet a lot more actual rejections than the average outside salesperson, who completes only 10 calls a day (the percentage of rejection, however, is no higher). And you must be adaptable: The mark of consistently successful salespeople is that they readily adapt to new markets, new people, new marketing strategies, and new products.

Understanding the other person won't hurt you, either. Why do people buy what they do, and from whom? What process do they use in deciding what to buy? How can you detect those processes when they occur?

Empathy, often described as the ability to walk in another person's shoes, is a valuable trait. One of the greatest double-play combinations in baseball used to spend their practice time before a game reversing roles. The shortstop would become the second baseman, and the second baseman would move to the shortstop's position. This gave each man a firsthand feeling for where he had to place his throw so that his partner could make a good pivot and throw to first base.

Can you do as much in your selling work? Good salespeople attempt it all the time, and the most successful ones come as close as anyone can to putting on that other person's shoes. Visit your customers at their locations and see how they use what you sell. Talking with prospects and customers, if done with an open mind and a willingness to learn, will reveal the way they think, the problems they face, and the need they have for you and your product. Talking to other salespeople can reveal what they know about how customers use your product. And can you use the product yourself, even if only on a trial basis? If your own company uses the product you sell, talk to the employees directly involved with it. If you approach your work with an open mind and the desire to be of service to others, you can determine what your prospects and customers think, feel, and need.

And you need enthusiasm. Would anyone want to buy something from you that you yourself were not excited about? It is unlikely. Enthusiasm also helps you face rejection. If you know the worth of what you sell, you can see that people who hang up on you or are rude or unresponsive have lost an outstanding buying opportunity. It is not something you take personally. You, at least, know the value of your product and work.

Salespeople can have a variety of selling styles. There is the hail-fellow-well-met salesperson, with a broad smile, several good stories, a pleasant word for everyone, and who is enjoyable to know. Such salespeople appear to make their sales primarily on the force of their personality, although the basics of good selling are never too far beneath the surface.

Another, equally successful, salesperson is the product-knowledge wizard. This seller knows every possible subtlety of the product and its uses and benefits, and simply cannot conceive of the prospect's buying something else—assuming the prospect is in his or her right mind. The sale here is made through a partly intuitive analysis of the prospect's needs and a persistent presentation of the product's benefits.

A third salesperson succeeds by combining elements of the first two approaches. This person is pleasant but businesslike. Through product knowledge, he or she is able to talk intelligently about the prospect's problems and be persuasive about how the product can solve them.

Whichever of these three broad (here oversimplified) types you resemble, or aspire to be, you can have something in common with all successful salespeople: the ability to establish rapport with your prospect. A sympathetic or harmonious relationship with a prospect better enables you to persuade someone to buy. A sale is the sum effect of empathy, enthusiasm, product and market knowledge, and a systematic selling plan. The way you make use of these elements makes you the unique salesperson you are.

Influencing Your Prospective Customer

You are not the only party to the sale who is unique. Each prospect is different, and for that reason, no two calls you handle will be the same. But we can make some generalizations about prospects' reactions to you when you call, reactions that not only determine how well you establish rapport, but ultimately whether you make sales or lose them.

Studies indicate that to your prospects, the most important factor in their contact with you as a salesperson is the interest you show in them as individuals and the concern you have for their problems. This is true whether they are direct consumers or business buyers. As much as one-half of the prospect's reaction to you will depend on this one perception—which is why so much emphasis is placed on your ability to empathize and establish rapport. The most significant element in your overall success at selling is the impression you create of your concern for the prospective buyer.

A second important factor is your credibility. The accuracy of the information you give is critical if you are to prevent misunderstandings and build trust. This factor can account for as much as one-fourth of the prospect's evaluation of you and your call. Do you make either subtle or obvious errors in your presentation? Do you contradict yourself at any step of the contact? Are you careless or glib? Do you give deceptive or evasive answers to tough questions from the prospect? Any of these practices can cost you sales. You must be accurate in what you say to your prospects.

What kind of impression do your speech habits make? These include not only your enunciation and pronunciation, but also your choice of words and how fast you talk. Up to one-fifth of the contact's reaction is to your speech habits and mannerisms, so they are well worth paying attention to. Strong regional accents can be a problem, especially if you must talk to prospects in all parts of the country (you may even have to deal with regional prejudices). Your speech, if you are careless, can offend prospects.

The fourth important factor is the overall impression you make. As much as one-fifth of the reaction you create is based on the image you project, even though you are selling on the telephone and not in the presence of the prospect. Sales professionals know that image counts, whether it is visible or not. Only you can determine if it will count for or against you.

In face-to-face situations we judge others by their appearance—the image they create—based on such factors as how well their clothing is suited to the work they are doing, how they carry themselves, and how they are groomed. The importance of your image as a teleseller doesn't disappear just because you aren't visible. Think of how often you create a mental picture of a person you can hear but not see—a radio announcer, for example, or a person in another room. You also do this when you are talking on the telephone. Well, you are being visualized, too. The prospect is forming a mental image of what you look like on the basis of things you say and do.

How does a prospect create an image of you? A lot of things give you away; when added up, they represent a composite picture of what you look like to the prospect. Some of these are obvious: voice, vocabulary, rate of speech, grammar, enunciation, any regional dialect you may have. Then there are subtler suggestions of your appearance: how professionally you answer the call or introduce yourself, for example; how well you conduct the interview; and what background sounds can be heard while you talk.

What about your personal mannerisms: Do you pay attention? Do you use slang or industry jargon? Are you sarcastic? Do you inject controversial subjects into the conversation, or make outlandish statements?

It is a good idea to ask yourself right now, "What kind of image am I projecting? How do I appear over the telephone?" Remember, as much as one-fifth of your possible success is riding on the impression you make, even on the telephone.

Draw up a list in the space below of the ways in which you "appear" on the telephone.

1. _____
   _____
2. _____
   _____
3. _____
   _____
4. _____
   _____
5. _____
   _____

The final element in the contact's reaction, accounting for perhaps another one-tenth, will hinge on courtesy: your being appropriately polite in your dealings with your prospect. The key word here is "appropriately." Your work does not call on you to be other than normally well-mannered. Excesses in either direction—either abrupt, curt, abrasive remarks and a condescending attitude, or, on the other hand, downright servility—will get you in trouble and will cost you sales.

These, then, are the factors that determine how prospects or customers react to you when you make contact with them. They evaluate you on the basis of:

- the interest you show in their problems and needs
- the believability of the information you dispense
- your speech
- the image you create for yourself
- your manners

Throughout this book we will come back to these elements. For now, memorize them. They are the backbone of the system of selling that you will be asked to make a part of your unconscious work habits.

Finally, you must consider how many times and over what period of time you will be in touch with a prospect. This will influence how much importance to place on the various aspects of the call and determine how much time you have to work on ensuring that you will be received positively.

Why People Buy

Who are you, and why did you buy this book? It would be safe to bet you are a person who holds one of three positions: sales manager, training director, or salesperson. Now, why did you buy this book? If you are a sales manager, you may want to encourage (or require, as sales managers are wont to do) a greater use of the telephone by your people in order to either increase sales or reduce costs—or both. If you are the training director, charged with the responsibility of training the sales managers' people, you ask, "Why reinvent the wheel? I'll assign this book and use my time to prepare for in-class activity." And if you are a sales representative eager to get ahead of peers and competitors, or to increase the rewards and satisfaction you receive from your work, you want to learn to make better use of the telephone in your selling.

These three buyers have five motives among them. Just what, exactly, is going on in the mind of your prospect when he or she decides to buy? You have already analyzed a prospect's reaction to your call. How do you make a sale in that context? Can you have an effect on the prospect that will induce a favorable buying decision? Can you close a sale?

To begin to answer these questions, it is important to first understand that people buy *benefits,* not *products.* Chapter 3 will present benefits-selling in detail, as a part of your task of acquiring product knowledge. How each prospect benefits will vary from one prospect to another, so the answer to the question is often complex. For now, keep in mind that *a benefit is what the prospect can expect to gain when he or she buys your product.*

We are not talking about gain in a narrow sense; "Gain" here refers to the psychological needs and desires that will be satisfied by the advantages your product offers—the psychological factors that come into play to prompt a person to make a buying decision. Once you have identified the buying motivation at work, you will know which of your product's benefits to stress in your sales presentation. For example, your home housecleaners are fully bonded (one advantage); they therefore provide *convenience* with *security* (two benefits). Or, your word processing equipment can manage five stations simultaneously (one advantage); it thus *saves money* (one benefit) by increasing productivity. By demonstrating how your product fulfills the buying motivation in terms of benefits, you will be able to close the sale.

One of the steps in your sales strategy is your analysis of the prospect's needs and desires. These fall into two categories: the "must-haves" and the "would-like-to-haves." For example, all law firms *must have* available a law library that is complete and current; all offices *must have* an adequate amount of the necessary supplies on hand to conduct their business. Your job in selling here is to determine which of the must-haves you can satisfy to the benefit of your prospect in order to make the sale.

The would-like-to-haves, or desires, are more subtle, and fulfilling them depends more on your selling creativity. For example, a car owner may be required by law to have liability insurance but the unique features of your automobile coverage, which may include guaranteed renewal, annual premiums, and claim service as near as a telephone, can all help you show the prospect that while they need protection, they *should like to have* yours over the competition's because of the added convenience and peace of mind you offer. In this case, you have stressed benefits that the prospect may not even have thought of when considering coverage. You have created a desire to buy.

Every buying decision, then, whether to satisfy a "must-have" need or a "want-to-have" desire, is motivated by something. It is therefore important to your success that you attune your selling to the buying motivation of each prospect.

What are the most common buying motivations? The list you compile will depend on your product and market.

One of the strongest motives at work on buyers, whether they are individual consumers, professionals buying for business, or key business executives themselves, is the desire for *financial benefit*. Financial benefit can come from making a purchase that will increase in value, such as real estate or a similar investment. It can come as a way to reduce costs, as when a company buys a faster data-processing system, or an individual purchases a new freezer to save on food costs by buying in bulk. Finally, financial benefit can be demonstrated when you show a prospective buyer how your product will increase sales, profits, or both for his or her business. Showing your prospect a financial benefit of the buying decision you are recommending will almost always elicit a favorable response.

Another important motivation to buy is the desire all of us have for *security*, whether physical, emotional, or financial. People want to know they are protected from the financial damage an unexpected loss can inflict on them, so they buy insurance. A business may spend millions to protect the information stored in its computers from theft or manipulation. If you can show a prospect how purchasing your product will bring more security to his or her life or business, you will have gone a long way toward closing the sale.

Convenience is important to busy people; it is thus a very strong buying motivation. Selling by telephone, you are in an excellent position to stress convenience in your sales message, especially when follow-up and service are important to the purchase. Your product, too, can offer convenience. It can be easier to operate or less prone to breakdowns, more certain in its performance or longer lasting than competing products. The benefits of your product that offer convenience should be emphasized in your sales message from the beginning.

Sex appeal can influence the decision to buy many products. Does a health spa sell physical fitness, sex appeal, or both? Can you tell them apart? Even cigarettes and alcoholic beverages are sold by promoting an image of masculinity or femininity. If you are selling structural steel components to bridge contractors, you may have trouble finding a sexual motive in the buying decision. But if you can find one, use it.

Fear as a motivation has long been used in selling. And it is a complex motive with many ramifications. The important thing here is to recognize your customer's fears and make them work *for* you by stressing such services as guarantees, or by stressing the large and well-trained service department your company offers. People fear they may look bad to friends or colleagues, or fall behind their competition, if they don't have a certain product or don't make a wise purchase. They may be afraid of making a large financial commitment, or of buying the wrong thing. The fear of a financial setback will motivate some people to invest in extended warranties or service contracts on such consumer goods as cars and appliances.

To keep fear from working against you, play up the size, history, and success of your company, as well as your personal and professional qualifications as a salesperson. Give the prospect a list of companies that use your product, whether they are clients of your consulting firm or the Fortune 500 buyers of your company's new office equipment. This is reassuring and quiets subjective fears that may stand in the way of a sale.

The *expectation of pleasure* or satisfaction can also motivate people to buy. Many people like to have the best, latest, or most of something. This is not to recommend that you overdo the use of superlatives in your sales talk. But you can respond to this motivation by stressing the ways your product will enhance the quality of their life.

Finally, there is the *desire for acceptance* or respect. Most of us want to earn the approval and admiration of our peers, loved ones, or colleagues. Certainly, no one wants to appear the fool, or to feel swindled. Nor do people want to learn they have bought the wrong thing or been persuaded to buy something they didn't need. If you stress how well suited your product is to their needs, and how others who have bought it have benefited from it, you will find that the almost universal desire to be accepted can increase your chances of making the sale.

You can easily learn to appeal to all of these motivations, individually or in concert, when you are selling to a single consumer, such as a homeowner. But the problem of first identifying and then influencing the motives of a business person or professional buyer can be a little more complicated. Consider, for example, the person who buys type composition and printing for a publisher. While you may be able to provide virtually error-free typesetting services and faster and less expensive printing, the firm's present supplier may have the record of good service and the close association that years of doing business with someone breeds. Thus, while the buyer may respond favorably to your presentation in terms of financial gain and convenience, he may ultimately be dissuaded by his fear of making a buying mistake and of losing the deep personal satisfaction he gets from doing business with an old friend. So while you may have offered satisfaction of a demonstrable business need, you did not make the sale because you failed to satisfy a strictly personal motive.

Once you have identified both the needs and the buying motivations at work on a prospect, you are in a good position to satisfy the must-haves and create the would-like-to-haves so essential to a sale. As you analyze your prospect's needs and desires, review in your mind the features and advantages of your product that best match those motives. In that way, you will be able to stress the benefits that will satisfy those motivations for the prospect.

Begin here to think specifically about your prospects and customers. What motivates them to buy? Why? And, how do you know? For example, security may be a strong motive among homeowners considering your housecleaning service. They are concerned that their valuables be safe from theft, their home free from burglary. They reveal this motive by their questions about your process of screening employees and your bonding procedures, or by their comments about security or safety. As you give thought to your prospective customers, fill in the following form:

Buying Motives at Work on Your Prospects

Buying motivation	Check	Why?	How does it appear?
Financial Benefit			
Security			
Convenience			
Sex appeal			
Fear			
Pleasure			
Acceptance			

SELF INVENTORY	Yes	No
1. I discipline myself to put in the time, energy, and work needed to be successful.	____	____
2. I know the mechanics of sales contact and apply them to the selling and buying process in my business.	____	____
3. I provide my prospects and customers with a needed and valued product.	____	____
4. I know and understand the buying motivations that apply to the product I am selling.	____	____
5. I maintain the highest ethical standards when representing my company and myself.	____	____

For Thought and Action

How do you measure up on the performance goals of this chapter, as tested above?

Now that you've completed Chapter 2, how are you going to change your work habits?

Before going on to Chapter 3, have you (a) determined what improvements will be necessary for you to induce a favorable prospect reaction? (b) identified which buying motivations you will address in your selling activity?

CHAPTER 3

How to Use Product Knowledge to Your Advantage

The Key

You have to know your products inside and out—their uses, markets, and competitive advantages—in order to sell them effectively. In addition, you must be able to describe the products in terms of how they benefit their owners. There are procedures you can follow to quickly and easily acquire all you need to know to sell any products. When you have completed this chapter, you will be able to distinguish your products' features and advantages from its benefits, and you will have begun developing a sales kit to use in your teleselling. But your learning won't stop there: The acquisition of product knowledge is an ongoing, lifelong process.

It is important enough to repeat: You must know your products before you can sell them. The more you know about your products and their uses—both those that were intended and those discovered by your customers additionally—the more success you will have in selling.

How to Find Product Information

Begin your search for information about your company's products right in your own company. Or, if you are the marketing representative for other companies, look to the producer as the best source of useful information. Inside people can give you insights into such things as durability, reliability, and serviceability, and they can tell you what has to be done to provide the service the products or their users require.

Product-development people can be the source of a wealth of information, since they can tell you what a product does and why. Such information may also be available in product sheets, booklets, or samples, and marketing or advertising departments may have produced ads or brochures that will prove useful to you. Collect copies of all such material to begin building a sales kit. The information must then be tailored by you to customers' needs, which may be unique to each sale.

You will also want to understand the services your company provides for its products. Will it be necessary for the customer to order or reorder supplies? What is the lead time required to fill an order for either the product or its supplies? How much training is needed to use your product, and what technical support is required? Do you offer either or both? What related products can you sell?

Another factor you may want to consider is how the history, policies, and record of reliability of your company can add credibility to your presentation. Is it appropriate to build part of your sales message around the trustworthiness of your product and its performance? Such phrases as "This piece of equipment has been in service with some users for over twenty years now," or "Over two million units have been sold to satisfied users," can add sales appeal, increase prospect confidence, and build credibility into your sales message. If any such factors apply to your product or market, research them and add applicable information to your product-knowledge data bank.

Don't get bogged down in excessive technical details, though. If a prospect who has no reason to be concerned with complex technical questions brings them up in an inappropriate context, ask yourself what motives are behind this. Is the prospect revealing a legitimate concern, perhaps a misunderstanding or the fear of buying the wrong product? If so, address the underlying motive you have identified and head off the inappropriate questions. With enough experience and understanding, you will be able to control difficult technical questions by anticipating them in your own comments and questions.

Finally, does your product have a life cycle? If, for example, you are selling textbooks to schools, you should keep track of the period during which they are current and when they are scheduled to be revised. Then you will be able to advise your customers that a new product is coming out. You will be providing good service and, no less important, keeping your competitors out.

Next, turn to outside related literature that is available on both the product and the market. Catalogs, product bulletins, company and industry newsletters, and updates are vital to you, as are more general publications. The following short list of some widely available sources may help you begin.

DIRECTORIES

All-in-One Directory (annual)
Gebbie Press, Inc.
Box 100, New Paltz, NY 12561
Lists 430 professional business publications, 2,900 trade magazines, and 360 farm publications, as well as daily and weekly newspapers, radio and television stations, and general and consumer magazines.

The Newsletter Yearbook/Directory
The Newsletter Clearinghouse
44 W. Market Street, P.O. Box 311, Rhinebeck, NY 12572

Identifies hundreds of newsletters and their contents, covering numerous subjects and industries in detail.

The Encyclopedia of Assocations (annual)
Gale Research Company
Penobscot Building, Detroit, MI 48226

Business Periodicals Index
Where to Find Business Information
Both from:
John Wiley & Sons, Inc.
605 Third Avenue, New York, NY 10158

All of these directories may be available in libraries.

PERIODICALS

Business Week (weekly)
McGraw-Hill, Inc.
1221 Avenue of the Americas, New York, NY 10020

The Wall Street Journal (daily, Monday through Friday)
To subscribe, write:
200 Burnett Road, Chicopee, MA 01021

You will find these publications on newsstands and in libraries, though you may want to subscribe to either or both.

REGIONAL PUBLICATIONS

There is useful general and professional reading published throughout the country. As an example, if you are selling in southeastern Pennsylvania you should, of course, read the *Philadelphia Inquirer,* and also look into the *Philadelphia Business Journal,* which is published weekly. Other publications in the area, such as *Focus* and *Corporate Monthly,* will help complete your grasp of local business or consumer activity.

Seeking out these publications is worth your while. Your telephone selling is apt to be on a regional or national basis rather than just local, and you will want to keep informed about activity in your entire market.
Your product does not exist in a vacuum. In order to sell professionally, you will want to know about the industry or community you are selling to. For example, if you are selling cleaning chemicals to industrial plants, knowing which companies are thriving and which are closing plants in your territory would help you in selecting where to make your selling effort. Or if you are

selling a product for homeowners, you may lose a golden opportunity if you miss the announcement that hundreds of rental apartments in one area are soon to be converted to condominiums.

Another aspect of acquiring product knowledge is learning how your product compares with the competition's. How is yours better? Does your product do something that the other company's can't? What? Equally important, where are you weak compared to the competition? If you know your weaknesses you will be better prepared to head off or minimize negative reactions.

An excellent source of such information is your present customer base, if you have one. Talk to the key people at several of your major accounts, or ask consumers who you know have bought your product about their experiences with it. Be open-minded, and listen to what you are told.

Finally, look into professional or manufacturing associations. There probably are marketing associations or local and regional consumer and business groups that can prove invaluable to you, not just for product and market information, but as sources of leads. The Encyclopedia of Associations will help you here; its information is broken down by interest and profession.

There is probably more than you want to know about your product and market available to you. You have to dig only a little to be overwhelmed. But if you feel there is information you need in order to sell effectively, dig it out.

Remember, the more calls you make and the more prospects and customers you talk with, the more you will learn. So don't wait until you have learned all there is to know before you get on the telephone. You will never make one call that way. Armed with the basics, make the calls. In most instances, you will find that you are the expert on your products and their uses. No matter how little you know, it is still more than the prospect is likely to know. Business buyers particularly, professionals themselves, look to you, the teleseller, as the source of the most complete information about your products and their applications.

Using Product Knowledge

What are you selling? Let's assume, for the moment, that you are working for USA National Life Insurance Company. "Why, I'm selling life insurance policies," you'd answer.

But let's be a little more imaginative and say you are selling provision for family financial needs in the event of the prospect's untimely death. Thus, you have strengthened your selling statement by supporting the *feature*, insurance on a life, with an *advantage* of that feature of your company's product. If you stopped your presentation there, you probably would not make the sale. Because what you are really selling, and have not yet stated, is financial security, peace of mind, and convenience. These are the *benefits* a prospect who decides to buy insurance is really looking for.

One of the most common shortcomings many tellsellers have, ranked right behind an ineffective analysis of needs and the fear of asking for the or-

der, is selling features and advantages instead of benefits. As a sales philoso-
pher put it, "You are not selling a half-inch drill bit, you are selling all the
benefits of a half-inch hole."

A *feature* is a description of the product in terms of its real or perceived
specifications. Features define what the product is, the characteristics that
combine to make it unique. Some features of different products might be:

PRODUCT FEATURES CHART

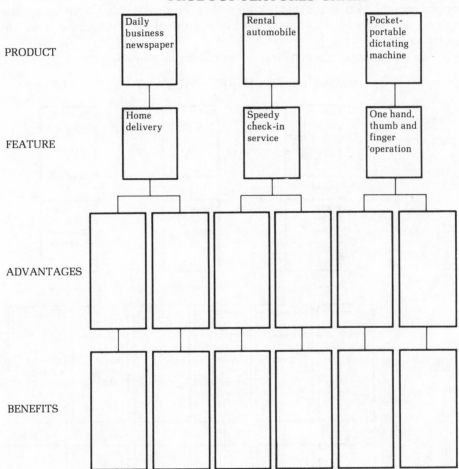

Select a product you will be selling on the telephone and write it here:

_____

Now, describe in two or three key phrases or sentences what the features of
that product are:

1. _____
2. _____
3. _____

An aspect of product knowledge that is of even greater interest to your prospect is the *advantages* each product feature produces. An advantage explains what a feature will do for the user. Each feature will have one or more advantages.

Returning to your role as a teleseller for USA National Life Insurance, what are the advantages to the prospect of this feature of your product: "guaranteed lifetime renewal protection" (the company cannot cancel the policy once issued)? At least two come to mind: First, coverage cannot be canceled for *any* reason. Also, since this feature makes physical condition irrelevant, the insured will not have to undergo periodic physical examinations to keep the policy in force.

We can now continue filling in the charts we started.

PRODUCT FEATURES / ADVANTAGES CHART

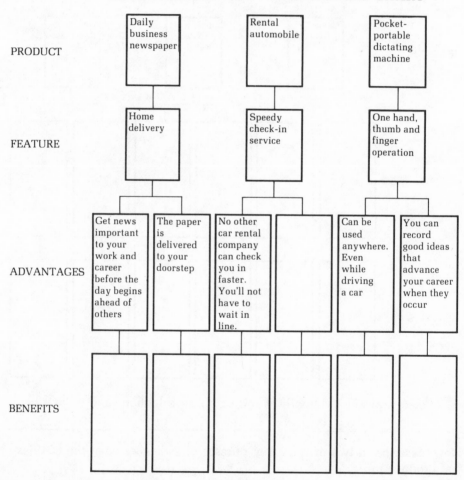

You will notice that every feature of the above chart has at least one advantage. You will find that very often features have several advantages.

Return to the list of product features you wrote down a few moments ago and write the second one you listed here:

_____

Using phrases and sentences, write at least two advantages the feature offers to those who would use your product:

1. _____

2. _____

3. _____

Remember, an advantage is a description of what the feature (not the product) does for the user.

The final, and key, element of product knowledge is learning the product's benefit to the user. Benefits are what the prospect or customer will gain

PRODUCT FEATURES / ADVANTAGES / BENEFITS CHART

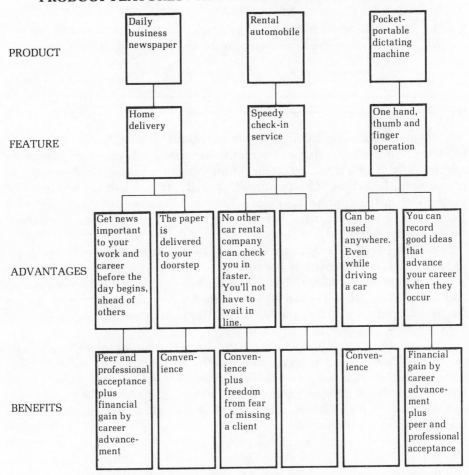

	Daily business newspaper		Rental automobile		Pocket-portable dictating machine	
PRODUCT						
FEATURE	Home delivery		Speedy check-in service		One hand, thumb and finger operation	
ADVANTAGES	Get news important to your work and career before the day begins, ahead of others	The paper is delivered to your doorstep	No other car rental company can check you in faster. You'll not have to wait in line.		Can be used anywhere. Even while driving a car	You can record good ideas that advance your career when they occur
BENEFITS	Peer and professional acceptance plus financial gain by career advancement	Convenience	Convenience plus freedom from fear of missing a client		Convenience	Financial gain by career advancement plus peer and professional acceptance

from the advantages of your product. In order to close a sale, you will need to make a connection between your product's features and advantages and the prospect's needs and buying motivations. That connection is the product's benefits.

How, then, does a prospect gain by having "guaranteed lifetime renewal protection"? Tying the benefit to buying motivations, you would stress that they no longer need fear being canceled. And they are free from the resulting inconvenience of finding new insurance. Don't forget the convenience that comes from being able to handle their insurance needs from their home, by telephone. Finally, they won't ever have to worry about their family's financial security.

The chart on page 27 lists several possible benefits of the other products presented; look over carefully before continuing. This will give you a feel for how advantages can be translated into benefits for all kinds of products.

Now, return to the advantages you listed on the preceding page. Select one and write it here:

_____

Identify the benefits the prospect will gain from this advantage. Remember, the benefit is produced by the advantage, not by the product or its feature.

    1. _____

    2. _____

    3. _____

Prepare a form like the one on page 27. Duplicate a sufficient quantity to be able to list the key features of each product you are going to sell. Begin by asking yourself which features are most important for the type of prospect you are going to be calling. Limit yourself, initially, to three to six features, and place them in the appropriate spaces. Go on to list the advantages that each feature has. Finally, list what benefits those advantages are likely to have to the prospects you will be calling.

Each feature is likely to have more than one advantage, and several advantages can be combined to produce one benefit. In other words, benefits-selling is not a mathematical exercise. It is a mental process whereby you mix and match what you know about your product with what you learn as you listen to each prospect. Over time, you will find your prospects also make their own contributions to your benefits list.

Now, ask yourself just what you should get across in the calls you handle. Which features, advantages, and benefits are essential to understanding the gain to be had from your product? In the beginning, keep to the basics, usually as stressed by your product sales literature. As you talk to prospects and customers, be alert to what *they* think is important. It may make you rethink the things you wrote down.

Of course, the most valuable aspect of your Features/Advantages/Benefits charts are the benefits boxes. Write out as many benefits statements as you can and begin committing them to memory. You will then have at your fingertips sales-closing information and a ready guide to benefits statements that you can easily refer to during a sales call.

Follow that by applying your knowledge to simulated sales situations. If possible, role-play sales call, to test yourself from a customer's point of view. What will you say if a customer asks a certain question? How does what you answered sound?

Product and market knowledge will also help you achieve credibility. Since you know what you are talking about, you will inspire trust and build the prospect's confidence in what you say.

There are other immediate dividends that come from knowing your product well. Regardless of the sales success of the call you are making at the moment, you will build respect for your professionalism that can pay off in the future. If you are selling to a prospect base that requires you to make repeated contacts, whether to close the sale in the first place or to service buyers, you will be remembered as a sincere business person who has the customer's interests at heart. You will meet objections more effectively. And, as your self-confidence grows, you will feel more and more comfortable making your calls.

If you are using the telephone to handle customer service, you gain additional benefits. As you increase your knowledge, you can renew excitement for your product among your customers, and thus resell them on continuing to use it. You can point out that they may be underutilizing it, and show them how to get even greater gains from their purchase.

You will see opportunities to sell in direct proportion to how much you know about your product and its uses. The pieces of information you gain from many different sources will all combine in a synergistic manner to make you an increasingly effective teleseller. You will speak with more conviction, handle calls more efficiently, and move more sales to a close.

The Sales Kit

To better enable you to use your newly acquired and expanding product knowledge at every opportunity, you should develop a sales kit. One of the advantages of telephone selling is that as you give your talk, you are able to refer to written notes and printed matter without distracting your prospect. Use the suggestions presented here with the understanding that they are guidelines to help you begin. Learn what works for you, and adapt your sales kit to the way you work.

1. *Keep it simple and easy to use.* Unlike outside salespeople, you cannot afford pauses in the conversation. You have to be able to put your hands on the information you need quickly.
2. *Be well-organized and consistent.* Begin by dividing your kit into sections, preferably by product or product category. If you use a descriptive brochure, make sure you put one at the head of each section of your kit. Follow that with only such backup data as you will need—not everything anyone would ever want to know about your product,

but what your experience and training tells you is likely to be important during the call. By using a uniform format throughout your sales
kit, you will ensure that you are not distracted from your presentation
because you can't find that missing piece of information.

3. *Use only marketing materials that work for you.* You should feel free
to tear apart the sales and marketing information you receive, and
reassemble it in a form that works for you. Discard what you find you
have no need for, and put the remaining material together in a form
that is easy to use.

4. *Let your experience on the telephone dictate your sales kit's content
and format.* As you make your calls, be alert to the kinds of information you use repeatedly. How can you organize your sales kit to con-
form to the pattern of your calls? What questions do you hear asked?
What objections do you encounter? What do your prospects say, and
when do they say it? How do they respond when you ask for the order? Keep the course and the content of your calls in mind while assembling a working sales kit.

5. *Keep it current.* Keep abreast of new developments in both your product and its market. As product improvements are introduced, additional uses identified, or new prospects uncovered, note them in your
sales kit immediately.

The most important items in your sales kit will be the Features/Advan-
tages/Benefits worksheets you develop. These worksheets will become the primary tool you'll use on the telephone. Therefore, be sure they are legible, and
in a location where you can put your hands on them immediately. At first, you
may want to put a check beside a benefit block each time you use that benefit
in a presentation. In that way, you will be able to tell which benefits are most
relevant for a product, and you can automatically integrate them into your
presentation. Or you may want to work the most frequently used benefit into
an attention-grabber (this will be discussed in Chapter 6).

It is also important to note when you find yourself saying, "I'll find out
for you and call you back." Each time you do, add the missing information to
your sales kit. Looking up the answer, thinking about it in terms of its benefit
to the prospect, and then writing it down will all help you remember what to
say the next time.

Again a word of caution is in order: Keep in mind that "if you get fancy,
you get beat." In identifying and stressing benefits, limit yourself to two or
three key benefits of each product you sell. You may learn all of the benefits
of each product, but don't overwhelm your prospect with them. Not only are
you likely to confuse the prospect, you may very well erode the credibility you
worked so hard to establish. In each call you handle, concentrate on what the
other party's buying motivation is, and present only the two or three benefits
that best satisfy that motivation. And, where appropriate, choose those benefits that give you a distinct advantage over your competition. Save all those
others you know for use in the other calls.

Stop now and think about the items you must have at your fingertips in order to conduct a smooth, professional, successful sales call. In the space below, or on a separate sheet of paper, compile a thorough list of things you will need to conduct the interview your call context or call goal dictates.

1. _____
2. _____
3. _____
4. _____
5. _____

Did you include all appropriate company worksheets and ordering instructions? How about information sheets for the products you will be presenting? Are appropriate responses to objections or scripted responses (if used) readily available?

Remember, KISS: Keep It Simple, Salesperson. Don't overburden yourself. If you have to shuffle through a mountain of materials and information, you will create barriers to communication with your prospect (this is discussed in detail in Chapter 11).

In addition to preparing yourself, your prospects may also have to be prepared to conduct an uninterrupted interview. What things should they have on hand so that they can talk knowlegeably with you? What will they need so they can make a buying decision at the end of the interview? At the appropriate point in the interview, perhaps after they have said they'll buy, you'll want to ask them to get what is necessary to conclude the call. Again, if such an activity applies to your selling situation, compile a list of those items your prospects should have on hand to enable you to close the sale and call.

1. _____
2. _____
3. _____
4. _____
5. _____

The prospect may need little or nothing at hand in order for you to be able to conduct an effective call. But by taking the time to get both yourself and the prospect ready, you ensure fewer interruptions and greater concentration on your sales message. To make it easier for you to set this up, stress to prospects that by taking a few minutes for them to get ready to discuss your product, you will take up less of their time and be able to give them the best service and recommend the most appropriate product. Finally, remember that if you must put a prospect on hold to get additional information, you should mention how long they can expect you to be away from the telephone.

Now that you are equipped with a good knowledge of your products and their uses, and have a sales kit that is organized to serve you, you are ready to make your first calls.

SELF INVENTORY	Yes	No
1. I am thoroughly acquainted with my company's products and what they do.	____	____
2. I translate product features and the resulting advantages into benefits for prospects.	____	____
3. My presentation to the prospect addresses what the product will do *for them*.	____	____
4. I assess the buying motivations of each prospect, and tailor my presentation accordingly.	____	____
5. All relevant sales literature is readily at hand for me to consult as needed while I am on the telephone with the prospect.	____	____

For Thought and Action

How do you measure up on the performance goals of this chapter, as tested above?

Now that you've completed Chapter 3, how are you going to change your work techniques?

Before going on to the Interlude and Chapter 4, are you at work on your planned acquisition of the product knowledge you'll need to sell effectively?

Interlude: A Special Activity

It's time to get on the telephone and sell. When you completed the activity in Chapter 1, page 9, what did you decide about where and how you want to use the telephone? Whom can you call to start getting that done? Don't stall! Take your prospect list and start calling. Work from 9:00 A.M. in two 3-hour shifts, with only an occasional break, to 5:00 P.M.

Keep a record of how many calls you make in a day. Approximately 60 business-to-business calls or 120 consumer-market calls should be your goal. Also note how many decision-makers you reach, how many actual sales interviews or presentations you make, if you close any sales, and what problems you encounter.

Remember, no matter how you do on your first day on the job, the sun will rise tomorrow, your family and friends still love you, and there will be more prospects for you tomorrow than there are today.

More important to your goals, once you have spent the six hours on the phone you are ready to read and learn *effectively* from this book. Even if you are successful on the telephone today, you can always be *more* successful.

CHAPTER 4

A Basic Sales-Call Strategy

The Key

> To sustain yourself in your teleselling career you must develop a basic call strategy that will serve you in all situations and help you achieve your call objectives, regardless of how they change. With time, the strategy will become part of your unconscious behavior, freeing you to respond naturally to each prospect. You can relax, confident that you'll remember to cover all the steps leading to the desired prospect action. This chapter will introduce you to a five-step call plan to aid you in your teleselling. You will be able to set goals for the number and length of your calls, and determine the best times to call your prospects

$\mathbf{A}$s you prepare to launch your teleselling campaign, have you done *all* your homework? What is your call strategy or plan? A carefully thought-out strategy is necessary if you are going to succeed at and get satisfaction from teleselling. Just picking up the receiver or plugging in your headset and calling people at random won't work.

The Selling Plan

Chapter 2 discussed the five factors that determine a prospect's reaction to a sales contact. They were given in order of importance. Can you list what the factors were, ranked from most to least important?

1. _____
2. _____
3. _____
4. _____
5. _____

Go back to page 16 to check your list if you are in doubt.

Look first at the most important factor: how you demonstrate your sincere interest in prospects, in their problems, needs, and concerns. Consciously or unconsciously, a prospect will listen for several clues. What questions do you ask? Do you ask them in order to learn the prospect's wants and needs? Do they help the prospect make an intelligent buying decision? Do you listen while the prospect is talking? Are you open-minded in your approach, never doggedly trying to sell something before you determine what the prospect needs? Do you project an attitude of helpfulness throughout the call, demonstrating a desire to serve, not sell? If you do all of this, you establish that you are interested in the prospect.

The believability of the information you impart is almost as important as your interest in a prospect. You want to be sure that your information is not misunderstood, and that the prospect doesn't feel misinformed, either of which can kill a sale. Information is judged by how accurate, complete, clear, and concise it is. Your product knowledge and basic selling and communication skills are important in projecting an image of truthfulness.

Your speech itself is being evaluated. The words you choose and your pronunciation are important, as are the pitch and tone of your voice and the rate at which you speak. While not as important as your demonstrated interest or the believability of your information, sloppy speech habits can put off a prospect. Remember, a failure to properly execute any of the mentioned points will result in your projecting a poor image of yourself.

Courtesy, like the impression you create, enters into the prospect's reaction to your contact with them. And, as with your impression, the telephone imposes some limitations and creates a few unique opportunities to demonstrate courtesy. There are things you can do to conduct yourself in a courteous manner. List the things you presently do, or can do, to project a polite image over the telephone:

1. _____
2. _____
3. _____
4. _____
5. _____

The first step in true courtesy is putting yourself in your prospects' place (empathizing). Your attitude should reflect your willingness to be of service to them in all of your dealings with them. More specifically, your list could include:

- answering the telephone promptly if you are handling incoming calls (The recommended policy is to answer after the first two rings but before four rings, if possible.)
- identifying yourself and your company right away
- expressing your willingness to be of service. For example, saying, "Yes, Mr. Wolfe, how may I help you?"
- being easy to talk to and deal with
- personalizing the call by using the prospect's name at every *reasonable* opportunity (Remember, you are not a friend. Keep it polite but formal.)

- showing your appreciation with such simple but often overlooked phrases as "thank you," or "I appreciate that"
- telling a person how long you will be when you put them on hold (Saying "I'll just be a second," then coming back on the line after several minutes will irritate people.)
- hanging up after the prospect does, if this is possible without being awkward

One precaution: Moderation is the best policy. Too elaborate politeness is likely to put off the prospect. Be naturally courteous, and you will get the favorable reaction you want.

Now that you know what factors in a call a prospect will react to, you want to use a selling system that will make that reaction a favorable one. A basic and simple call strategy that applies to all situations and contexts and can become part of your unconscious behavior will get the response you want.

Call Strategy and the Purpose of the Call

Each sales interview provides an opportunity to close a sale. As the tele-seller, it is up to you to guide the course of the call to that end. In order to move from the rapport you begin to establish with your initial hello, to the close of a sale before you say good-bye, you will need to follow a call strategy that will serve you in every call you handle.

What do you want to accomplish? Are you "cold calling" the universe for people you suspect may be prospects? Qualifying these prospects further? Making appointments? Servicing customers? Or are you doing follow-up selling to your regular buyers?

Once you have established your goals, you will employ a time-tested, systematic, and logical method of controlling the sales interview. The system naturally leads the prospect through a planned, step-by-step conversation, minimizing objections. This strategy can work for you whether you are making a one-call close or a multi-call sale.

The plan consists of 5 steps.

To begin, you get the prospect's complete (1) *Attention* by using an opening remark that stresses benefits. You go on to (2) *Analyze* needs and build interest through questioning. You then create a desire or need to buy with your (3) *Action-getting presentation* and by persuasively (4) *Answering objections* that arise. When you (5) *Ask for the order*, it comes as a natural conclusion to your call.

You will notice that each step's label began with an A. Use this as a memory aid.

When you follow such a selling plan, you get the information you need to determine which product you are going to present and how. You can then stress its most relevant benefits to the prospect. This will increase the odds of your making a sale.

Your call strategy should be easy to remember so that you can begin to use it immediately. With repetition it will come so naturally that you won't have to consciously think about it, but will be able to concentrate on using the selling skills you have acquired.

THE 5-STEP PLAN

1. *The Attention-grabber.* This is designed to get your prospect interested in listening to your further. In teleselling, it is estimated that you have about 20 seconds for this vital step. Unless you have made an appointment in advance, you are no doubt interrupting the person you are calling. You must get a lot of impact into what you say immediately after introducing yourself. So the importance of your attention-grabber cannot be overstated.

2. *Analysis of the prospect's needs.* Effective selling requires that you know your prospect's needs so you can show that what you offer will satisfy them. Through questioning and listening, you also build interest and start to create a desire or need to buy.

   If you are planning to work from a script, you will have to give a lot of fore-thought to your prospect's likely needs, and work them into the prepared presentation in advance.

3. *The Action-getting presentation.* This is where you emphasize your product's benefits that will satisfy the needs your analysis has uncovered. Only when prospects see *what's in it for them* do they make a favorable buying decision.

4. *Answering objections.* Unless you are the sole source of something everyone needs for survival, people are going to raise objections to buying what you are selling. Answering these objections is the fourth step in your selling strategy. Here, you are again persuading the prospect to buy, removing any obstacles that may exist.

5. *Asking for the order.* If you have effectively followed the first four steps, by asking for the order you will get the sales action that motivates the call. The prospect becomes a customer.

If your interaction with the prospect-turned-customer does not end with the close, or you are exclusively a customer-service teleseller, you might want to add yet another "A": the *Application of a service attitude.* After the sale is made, you will cement a lasting favorable relationship by taking pains to ensure smooth order fulfillment and user satisfaction. Applying a service attitude at all points of prospect and customer contact will keep your hard-won customers among your active accounts.

To review: You call the prospect and get Attention with an opening comment. You then have to Analyze his or her needs. An Action-getting presentation of the product you recommend follows. Answer any objections that arise, and Ask for the order. Finally, if applicable, Apply a service attitude in all of your dealings with your prospects and customers. Once the 5-step (or 6-step) strategy becomes automatic behavior, you will be a master of the basics of selling. Then, practice, practice, practice, and you will close more and more sales.

And don't let anyone tell you you are going to make every sale: not your manager, your marketing department, other sales people, trainers, nor even yourself. You aren't. Not even to qualified prospects. In the face of failure that at times seems overwhelming, you will nonetheless need to keep on going. Enthusiasm is the spark that helps you here. Don't let missed sales diminish your self-respect or your respect for your company and its products. Enthusiasm is a characteristic of *every* successful sales professional.

Perhaps the best summary for applying a call strategy to the purpose of the call is to do it.

What marketing activity are you going to undertake on the telephone?
_____

What is your objective in this activity? _____
_____

Tell what role each step of the 5- or 6-step strategy plays in helping you achieve that goal:

Attention-Grabber: _____
_____

Analysis of Needs: _____
_____

Action-Getting Presentation: _____
_____

Answering Objections: _____
_____

Asking for the Order: _____
_____

Applying a Service Attitude: _____
_____

You now have an idea of what use you want to make of each of the necessary steps in a good sales call. If you follow this strategy, making necessary adjustments and eventually having it become a part of your unconscious mind, you will be able to concentrate on the job of responding to each call naturally, confidently, and successfully.

Related Considerations

No presentation of the principles of a basic call strategy would be complete without considering the three most frequently asked questions about teleselling procedures: How many calls or sales contacts can one make in a day? How long should the typical call last? When is the best time to call?

The number of sales contacts you should expect to make in a day will depend on various factors:

The marketing context you are working in and your call objectives. If you are calling a list of suspects to qualify them as prospects, you will not need as much time per call as if you were conducting full presentations.

The quality of the list of names you are calling and how suitable they are to your call objectives. Working from a telephone directory to sell to a homeowner or parent, you may complete a lot of calls, but conduct few full presentations. But if you are calling a list of known customers to sell a pricing special, each call will take longer.

The product you are marketing, its complexity, and how much you must determine specific prospect needs in order to know which of a range of products to recommend. If you are selling a set of books on a subscription basis, using a script and offering a free gift to buyers, you can complete more calls than if you are required to qualify a prospect in order to determine which of your product models is best suited to his or her needs.

Other factors. These can include the paperwork you have to do following each call, and the amount of information you need to conduct the interview and its availability. Below you will find a Call-Length Checklist and Call-Results Form that you should use to help you plan your work.

CALL-LENGTH CHECKLIST

1. What marketing context are you working in?
   _____ cold-calling suspects
   _____ qualifying prospects
   _____ closing sales
   _____ providing customer service
   _____ other _____

2. What is your call objective?
   _____ to come up with a list of qualified prospects
   _____ to qualify prospects for appropriate sales literature
   _____ to make a full action-getting presentation to a decision-maker
   _____ to ask for an order
   _____ to solve customer-service problems
   _____ other _____

3. How good is your list of names in relation to your objectives?
   _____ a broad, unqualified suspect list
   _____ a list of prospects to be qualified further
   _____ a targeted list of qualified prospects
   _____ a clean list of known users of the product
   _____ other _____

4. How long should it take you to:
   _____ quickly screen suspects to produce prospects?
   _____ make a full presentation to qualified prospects?
   _____ ask decision-makers contacted for their order?
   _____ other _____

5. How many minutes will each goal-successful call take?

_____ 5 minutes

_____ 10 minutes

_____ 15 minutes

_____ 20 minutes

_____ other _____

6. How many hours will you reasonably be able to put in per day on the telephone?

_____ 3 hours

_____ 5 hours

_____ 7 hours

_____ other _____

Dividing the answer to question 5 above into your answer to question 6 (converted into minutes) will give you a preliminary answer to the question of how many calls to make in one day. However, go immediately to the form below and begin to track your results. Your actual on-the-telephone experience will eventually provide you with the accurate answer to this question. Make a copy of this form, duplicate it, and begin filling it in each day you work. Over a period of time, even as little as a week, you will have an idea of what you can reasonably accomplish.

Weekly Call-Results Form

Teleselling activity	Mon	Tues	Wed	Thurs	Fri	Totals
Calls dialed						
Qualifying information obtained						
Targets contacted						
Active presentations made						
Ask prospect to act						

You should, of course, continually evaluate your work, looking for ways to increase your productivity. Can you change your attention-grabber, be more efficient in screening prospects, or take a worthwhile shortcut in your planned call course?

After a week of work, establish a goal for the number of calls you handle in a day. Then keep on the telephone until you reach or exceed the goal. After a month, as you become more adept at handling calls, you can increase your goal. In any event, don't fall short of your goal for any period of time (unless your experience shows it was unrealistic in the first place). Discipline yourself to complete the job, which means hitting your call goal every day you work on the telephone. Use success to motivate you to even greater productivity. Try to exceed your previous daily, weekly, or monthly high.

Closely related to the question of how many calls you can make in a day is the matter of how long the average call should last. This will depend on your call objective. In a teleblitz—a large number of interviews made up of three or four key questions, to identify qualified prospects from a list of suspects or general prospects—the calls are usually short. A teleseller at a travel agency may teleblitz suspects from a bought list of travel-magazine subscribers, asking how frequently trips are taken, when the next one is planned, where to, and (to prospects who meet preestablished guidelines, such as a trip planned within the next six months) if the person would like to be presented with several outstanding opportunities from the agency.

Close qualifying, followed by a full action-getting presentation, answering objections, and asking for the order can take longer. The travel agent may call back to find out more about the just-qualified prospect's preferred activities, modes of travel, previous trips, choice of accommodations, types of experiences desired, and budget guidelines. Remember, though: No matter how extensive your presentation will be, you have only a few seconds in which to grab a prospect's attention. If you do that successfully, you can then take the time you need to achieve your call objectives.

But do keep in mind that telephone calls are thought of as shorter encounters than talking face-to-face. You are expected to be brief. If you go beyond 20 minutes (and you should, when possible, make your calls much shorter than that), you are not likely to be effective. The prospect's attention will wander or his or her irritation will rise. Keep it brief.

When is the best time to call prospects? Many salespeople develop an elaborate rationale when trying to figure out the best time. In the morning, they will allow business prospects time to get their desks cleared and have their first cup of coffee. Then, of course, there is lunch. And if you call after 4:00 P.M., the prospect will be busy completing the day's workload. Consumers can't be called while getting children and spouses off to school and work, breakfast dishes cleaned, or dinner prepared. They can't be called in the evening for fear of interrupting dinner. Call between dinner and bedtime, but don't call on Tuesdays because. . . . And so on and on. If you added up all these reasons not to call, you would conclude that there is less than one hour a day in which to make calls. And if the day is Wednesday, the week is practically shot. Oh well, maybe next week. . . .

Come on! The best time to begin calling is *now!*

Of course, some common-sense guidelines apply to each market. But these should not stop you from picking up the telephone right now—within reason, of course. You don't want to call too early, say before 8:30 A.M., or too late, after 9:30 P.M. Other than that, it is "store's open."

Business people often aren't in, or don't answer their telephones, before 9:00 A.M. or after 5:00 P.M. But even that isn't an absolute, and it may pay to try calling earlier or later. If you call someone when their work cannot be interrupted, you should make an appointment to call back at a more convenient time.

Most consumers cannot be called before 8:30 A.M. or after 9:30 P.M. without risking disturbing them and ruining your chances for a sale. If, when you do get through, you interrupt some important household activity, make an appointment, or announce when you will call back: "I'm sorry to have interrupted your dinner. I'll get back to you in one hour, when you have a few mintues to talk."

If you repeatedly have trouble contacting a business person, remember that what you are calling about is important to that prospect too, so make an appointment to call back. Find out from the person screening calls when you could reach the prospect.

Get on the telephone at the start of your work day and keep at it until the day is over. Make the necessary adjustments, using appointments, call-return messages, or just calling back, as your experience dictates. Don't waste time finding excuses not to call.

SELF INVENTORY   Yes   No

1. My call objective is clear in my mind before I pick up the telephone.   ____   ____

2. I recognize the need to guide and direct each call to the conclusion I desire.   ____   ____

3. I know what I am going to say after I say hello.   ____   ____

4. I use a logical sales plan to help me get to my call objectives.   ____   ____

5. I am prepared to make a sale in each situation I encounter.   ____   ____

For Thought and Action

How do you measure up on the performance goals of this chapter, as tested above?

Now that you've completed Chapter 4, how are you going to change your technique?

Before going on to Chapter 5, have you committed the 5-step sales-call strategy to memory?

CHAPTER 5

Prospecting

The Key

> The purpose of prospecting is to reduce the world at large to a list of those most likely to buy from you immediately or in the near future, and to do it quickly and efficiently. While much of this activity goes on before you make your telephone call, prospecting begins in earnest once you get a suspect on the line. When done correctly, prospecting allows you to spend a majority of your selling time where it will do the most good: talking to those who have a current need for your product. As you read this chapter, concentrate on how the techniques presented apply specifically to you. Once you have learned how to identify decision-makers and get through to them when you call, you can set up record-keeping procedures to begin measuring your results.

So there you sit, by the telephone. You know your products well enough to talk knowledgeably about them with others. You have a call strategy in mind that will enable you to close sales. You are ready. But whom, among the more than 225 million people in the country, are you going to talk with?

Knowing Whom to Call

For most salespeople, prospecting is probably the hardest part of selling. You begin work excited about your product and wanting to sell it. All your product knowledge leads you to think of it as the best available. Prospects should need only to be told about it to buy it.

Then you begin to make your calls and you suddenly learn that not everyone who should be interested in your product will even talk with you. Some are downright rude to you. As you make your way from the more than 225 million individuals in this country to the ones among them who will buy from you, you will encounter a lot of rejection—most of it in the prospecting phase.

When you realize the percentages involved, you see what you are up against. If you were to start from scratch, you would have to contact 50 people to produce 1 suspect. For every 3 suspects you uncover, 1 will be a prospect.

From every 3 prospects, 1 will be a "qualified" prospect, that is, in the market for your product at the time of your contact. And, among 3 qualified prospects, you will close 1 sale. As you can see from the table below, you are faced with contacting approximately 450 people to close 1 sale.

Prospecting as a Numbers Game

Selling activity	Number of calls			
Cold calls to produce a suspect	1	50	150	450
Suspects to produce a prospect	0	1	3	9
Qualified prospects to close	0	0	1	3
Closes	0	0	0	1

Remember that your main objective is to produce as large a prospect list as possible. But the first step in prospecting need not take a long time. Your first job is to narrow a large undifferentiated universe—the entire country, all retail clothing outlets, the city of Cincinnati—down to "suspects." Suspects are, first, people who should want or need your product. Second, and equally important, they have the available financial resources to buy your product. Finally, they have access to your channel of distribution.

If you are just starting out, you will find help in the form of mailing lists, available from firms that specialize in compiling or managing them. Especially valuable as a source of such firms is the Standard Rate & Data Service's publication *Business and Consumer Direct Mail Lists* (5201 Old Orchard Road, Skokie, IL 60077).

Another source of suspect names is special-interest-publication subscriber lists. In the *All-in-One Directory*, published by Gebbie Press, you can find, for example, a total of twenty-nine magazines addressed to *key* people in the food industries. *Cereal Chemistry* has 4,000 subscribers; *World Coffee and Tea*, over 10,000. If your market is all food processors, there are over 526,000 subscribers to the 29 publications listed (of course, some of them will be duplications). You can contact the circulation department of any publication whose subscriber list you are interested in. The circulation manager will tell you if the list is available, from whom (if not from them), and if it can include telephone numbers. Do check the reputation of any list vendors or publications whose lists you are contemplating using—and in the case of vendors, where the lists you are getting come from. Ask for and consult references. How did a list do for the referenced users? Was its use close enough to your intentions to give you any insight into how it will do for you?

Telephone numbers are often available at a slight extra charge, and there are also telephone number look-up services available.

If you are selling to businesses, one useful tool may be the Standard Industrial Classification (SIC) number. This is a categorization of business according to primary activity. Almost every industry has one, including nudist camps (#7032) and Ping-Pong parlors (#7999). Learn the SIC numbers of your target audiences so that you can more readily identify them when looking for mailing lists or studying the demographics provided by such agencies as your state's department of labor and industry or your local chamber of commerce. You can find a list of all SIC numbers in *The Standard Industrial Classification Manual,* available from the U.S. Government Printing Office, Washington, DC 20402.

Finally, don't rule out the use of the telephone to help you qualify suspects. For example, you may be interested in selling to eyeglass manufacturers who offer a line of children's frames. But the only list available is for all eyeglass manufacturers. A teleblitz of such a list, with two or three key questions, can result in a list of known prospects in a short time. The telephone is ideal for such work: faster and more accurate than the mail, more cost-effective than conducting in-person interviews.

All right. Either through responses to or follow-up on mailing campaigns using your lists, advertising responses, or a teleblitz campaign, you have identified most of those among the suspects who are legitimate prospects, people who should have an immediate need or desire for a product like yours. You probably identified them because through their behavior, they fall into one of the following groups, being people who:

- have bought similar items in the past
- are involved in some activity that indicates they may buy
- have responded to your (or a competitor's) advertising and promotion

Again, mailing lists are a good source of prospects who have some or all of these characteristics. You may find lists broken down into numerous applicable categories:

People or businesses that have bought products like yours in the past. Such lists are appropriate if the product is expendable, needs to be resupplied, is such that owning one does not preclude owning others, or is suitable for replacement.

People or businesses involved in specific activities that you know make them likely buyers of your product. Members of health spas or country clubs may be in the market for sporting goods, or wealthy enough to want your high-fashion magazine. Newly incorporated small businesses need office supplies or services. Sales managers with even the largest corporations may be able to use your product as a premium, or your service as a means of reducing their cost of sales.

People or businesses that have responded to an advertisement. Anyone who has ordered a new subscription to a home-improvement magazine is a likely prospect for a variety of products, from tool sets to how-to books. A company that just requested free information on how to do presentations may be in the market for your business-communication consulting service or your audio-visual merchandise.

Do you keep in touch with existing customers, servicing their needs, recommending new applications for your product, and upgrading sales to newer or better products? It would be a serious mistake to take such people for granted. Your competition doesn't.

You should also keep former customers in a diary for appropriate regular contact. You may be able to sell them new benefits that arise from improvements in your product (or from additions to your product knowledge). If you don't keep in touch, you will never know when they grow dissatisfied with your competitor. Remember: The most likely source of new sales is your own customers, both current and former.

The checklist below will help you begin to identify your own sources of suspects. Consider each source, note if it has any value to you (by "yes," "no," or some more elaborative annotation such as "much," "some," or "little"), and think about how you will go about tapping that source. Then draw up a plan to get suspects from each applicable source.

Sources of Suspects: A Checklist

Sources	*Value*	*Plan/Comments*
Customer file		
Inactive accounts file		
Mailing lists		
SIC Directories		
Telephone directories		
Cold calling		

You have come a long way in a short period of time. You have moved from a pool of over 225 million people to a point where you are ready to make a sales presentation and ask for an order.

Pre-Call Research

In business-to-business selling, especially with more complex products or in a situation that requires more than one or two calls, your prospecting may include some degree of initial and ongoing research and data gathering. This pre-call research is to acquaint you as thoroughly as possible with the prospect company, the person (or persons) involved in the buying decision, and the buying process.

The extent of this research depends on the *context* of the call in your marketing plan and your call goals. Are you trying to develop leads? Are you calling to draw attention to your company or product, or to pave the way for an in-person visit? Are you trying to refine your analysis of needs, so you can more persuasively present the right product from your line? Are you putting the finishing touches on a live product presentation? Is this a service call? Or are you going to attempt to close a sale you have been working on?

Knowing the marketing context of your telephone call and what you want to accomplish tells you what you have to learn about the prospect or his or her company before you call.

If you are selling to homes rather than businesses, what kind of information do you need? A consumer's income level? Marital status? Whether the prospect is a home owner? His or her age, occupation, number of children? Pets? Recent major purchases? The list may seem endless. Control it by concentrating on what really matters.

As many questions accompany business-to-business teleselling.

What do you need to know about a company before you call? Its size, whether as revealed by assets, sales volume, or number of employees? What kind of business they are in? What types of equipment they use? How they market what they make? If their credit rating is acceptable?

How does a company produce or service its product? Is it mass produced, produced on a cycle (like clothing), or produced on demand? Are they experiencing increased or diminishing demand? Where does what you are selling fit in? Make a list of the information you need, item by item.

Where can you find the information needed? Several possible sources come to mind:

a. You may already have helpful files at your work station to get you started.
b. Records may exist within your own company that will give you information.
c. It may be helpful for you to talk with some of your known contacts at the prospect's place of business, or to similar people from among your customers.
d. The business section of your local library may contain useful sources of information.
e. Your own past experiences with others like the prospect or the company you are attempting to sell may help.

Add the sources of each item to your compiled list.

Prospecting Techniques

Once you have made a card file with the names of the individual consumers or companies you intend to call, perhaps the person within each company you want to talk with, and all necessary information, get back on the telephone and begin selling. Plan to make the maximum use of calling time. Develop a work plan to make good use of your time on the telephone by doing all your preparation and follow-up during non-calling hours.

At the end of the day, or before your first call in the morning, review your prospect cards. Plan to call a sufficient number of prospects to make a full day's work. Figure on 10 calls an hour for business-to-business selling, 20 in a consumer market or other teleblitz campaign. Of course, as you gain experience, adjust the hourly goal. The 10 or 20 calls per hour recommended here is based on experience in a variety of markets. Resist the temptation to lower the goal.

Have your prospect cards in whatever order you find appropriate: alphabetically, by industry, by location, or by some particular attribute. Then work your way through the cards in the order your plan dictates. Don't be tempted to jump around just because some of the calls don't work out to your satisfaction. The old adage, "Plan your work and work your plan," applies here, as it does most places in selling. If you fall into the bad habit of dropping your plan and then eventually not making a plan, you won't survive the long run. Refer back to the chart on page 44. How many calls do you have to make to close a sale or reach your other goals? How many sales do you have to make to reach your quota? How much extra can you make by exceeding your quota? How long will it take you to do that?

With your first telephone call you are likely to encounter two substantial problems that deserve special attention and preparation on your part: The first of these, almost exclusively the concern of business-to-business tellsellers, is getting through the call screens set up within companies. The second problem, characteristic of both consumer and business teleselling, is determining who has the authority to buy.

Getting through to the person you want to talk with is known as penetrating the screen. The screen is typically composed of a switchboard operator and the decision-maker's secretary. Experienced tellsellers will tell you that trying to penetrate a screen is their most frustrating task.

But there are general procedures to help you penetrate screens. They vary with your goals, your market, and your personality, and those of your prospect. It will be appropriate to behave one way if you are making a one-call close with no likely follow-up contact regardless of the outcome of the call, and another way if you are trying to establish a long-term selling relationship with your contact. In addition, you must give thought to what behavior you are comfortable with. The four techniques described here will not work for all people in all situations, but there is one that will work for you in your situation.

Plowing through the screen. Your attitude and behavior reflect your conviction that no one can stop you. You assume your best "voice of authority." Keep the screeners off balance by closing your answer to every question they pose with a counter-question. All this is aimed at convincing them of the urgency of your talking with the prospect, or at intimidating them into putting you through.

When you are asked, "What is this in reference to?" you can be vague, even deceptive, and still be successful. Don't forget to end your answer with the question, "Is he [or she] in?" You should expect this method to alienate those guarding the screen. But if your call is a one-call close with no follow-up, you may decide that the prize in this case is worth the price. Or you might answer the question with one of your best benefit statements, phrased in such a way as to make it seem as though the screener would be remiss if you were not put through. For example, if you got the decision-maker's name from a list of known buyers of a related product, you might say, "He expressed interest in our technique for increasing levels of productivity. Is he in?"

Going around the screen. Build a sense of urgency and need. But don't tip your hand to the extent that the screener makes the buying decision for the decision-maker. The best technique for going around the screen is to rework a benefit statement in such a way as to make it a *benefit to the screener* to let the decision-maker talk with you. Write out one or two of your earlier benefits statements in a way that makes it a benefit to the screener to put you through to the decision-maker. Try them, revise them, and try them again. Keep the ones your experience shows work, revise or scrap the ones that don't.

Going above the screen. Going above the screen may require more extensive pre-call research and necessitate a more elaborate pre-call marketing strategy. But the technique is very effective in large organizations, and can serve you well in medium and small businesses as well. Through research, identify the highest-ranking officer in the company who is likely to benefit from buying your product. Call or write that person, presenting introductory information stressing benefits. Inform the executive that you will be calling to discuss this important subject in greater detail in a few days. Begin your tele-selling account-penetration with the promised call, or with a cold call. You know you are likely to be referred to a lower level of the company, and you are ready. Calling the senior vice president of finance, you fully expect to be told to call the head of management of information systems to talk about your new money- and time-saving products. Now you are in a position to call the information systems manager and tell the ever-present secretary, the ultimate screener, that you were talking with the vice president of finance (or use his name), and he told you to speak with Ms. Jackson before getting back to him.

If you use this strategy, be on your guard that you don't get bounced too low in the decision ladder. You want to know, in advance if possible, who really makes buying decisions. If they rely on suggestions from other decision-makers, you must involve all the concerned parties in the process. Again, the telephone facilitates your doing this with both calls and follow-up correspondence. Avoid the situation where you have persuaded a non-decision-maker to buy the product. Then you are in the very unsatisfactory position of having a subordinate in a prospect or customer company trying to do your job for you—sell your product. You are the expert. The other person will not sell as effectively as you can, nor even know how to sell. He or she almost certainly won't go out on a limb with the employer in order to close your sale. It is very tempting to talk with anyone who will listen, but know where to draw the line, and don't go below the decision-maker.

Go below the screen. This technique is especially effective with those prospects to whom you will have to make many calls. It involves establishing a rapport with the screener.

1. Learn the person's name and use it.
2. Involve the screener in your process. Begin doing this in your intro-

ductory call or letter. End the announcement of your forthcoming call with a statement like, "Next week I will call your secretary to arrange an appointment for a half hour of your uninterrupted time on the telephone."

3. Finally, be sincerely cooperative in your dealings with the screener in all the calls you make to close the sale and service the account.

Experience has shown that involving the person who screens the decision-maker's calls is the most effective technique in the long run. Your further reward will be those situations where the screener cooperates with you, giving you valuable inside information that actually helps you sell to the company.

You can evaluate your productivity by using the Weekly Progress Report below, which will help you distinguish among calls completed, screens encountered, decision-makers reached, and presentations to decision-makers made. In this way you can determine a pattern of likely success to be expected at each level. Remember, industry-wide experience shows you will be successful at penetrating the screener in 1 out of 3 cases. If you aren't doing that

Weekly Progress Report

NAME: _____   WEEK OF: _____

Day	Total calls	Contacts with deci- sion-makers	Presen- tations completed	Total prospects	Prospects ranked			Refer- rals re- ceived*
					A	B	C	
Monday								
Tuesday								
Wednesday								
Thursday								
Friday								
Totals								

---

* A note about the referral column to the right on the chart. Another potential source of prospects is your customers. If you have just closed a sale, completed a presentation that went well without resulting in an order, or finished servicing a customer, ask the other party for referrals to others who may be interested in your products. A textbook teleseller could ask, "Professor Huxtable, who else in the Anthropology Department teaches Cultural Anthropology? Would they consider using our text, with its strong emphasis on the biological bases of behavior?" The representative of a photography studio could ask, "Mrs. Miller, would others in your neighborhood [or family] benefit from our special offer?" Prepare a request for referrals statement to include in your sales call wrap-up strategy, and use it. Keep track of the number of referrals that result.

well, reconsider both the strategy you chose and what you are saying. Don't get discouraged. Just improve on what you do and say. And keep calling.

The other frequent problem you encounter, that of identifying the decision-maker in a buying situation, can be just as frustrating. It is important for you to know who is in a position to make the final buying decision. You don't want to make a full presentation, in one or several calls, only to learn that someone other than the person you have been speaking with will have to be persuaded before the purchase can be made. That other person is the one you should have been talking to in the first place. If you succeed in persuading the wrong person to order your product, it can result in cost and inconvenience to you and others in your company. You can be virtually certain the product will be returned or the order canceled once the real decision-maker learns of the sale. You have lost not only money, but a lot of good will as well.

Identifying the decision-maker in a business can be a complex process. It may well be more than one person, requiring you to work vertically in a hierarchy, or horizontally among a committee of peers whose departments are affected by the buying decision. But often the best way to find out is simply to ask a direct question: "Do you make that decision, Mr. Johnson? Alone, or with the concurrence of others?"

If you determine that the decision-making process is complex, or if you are having difficulty getting a clear picture of the situation, review these points and apply them to your situation:

1. While processes and key individuals can vary from industry to industry, within the same industry the processes are likely to be the same or similar. Refer to your experience with similar companies to guide you.
2. By starting as high in a hierarchy as possible, if you are bounced to a lower level, you have opened the door with the higher authority for follow-up.
3. The records in your company's files may help. Especially if your prospect is a former customer, or if you are trying to increase sales to an existing customer, previous records may give you the insight you need.
4. It may be helpful to talk with other tellsellers who have experience with prospects like yours.
5. Job titles can be a good indicator of the authority hierarchy in a company. What do the titles of the parties involved tell you?

If you are selling to consumers, again, your best strategy is to ask direct questions: "Mrs. Morris, is this a purchase you decide on? Do you consult any other member of the household?" Use the latter question *only* if you sense it is absolutely necessary. You don't want to start Mrs. Morris thinking, "I'd better check with John before I say yes," and thus kill a sale.

Whatever product you are selling, and regardless of the market, identifying the decision-maker is always necessary and sometimes difficult. Be prepared to dig a little for the information you need. It will pay off in increased sales.

SELF INVENTORY	Yes	No
1. I take the time to do needed research before calling a prospect.	____	____
2. I use the knowledge my research provides to establish rapport with the prospect.	____	____
3. I know whom I should talk with, by name or title, before placing the call.	____	____
4. I make sure I am talking to the person with the authority to buy before continuing the contact.	____	____
5. My efforts to get through to decision-makers are usually successful.	____	____

For Thought and Action

How do you measure up on the performance goals in this chapter, as tested above?

Now that you've completed Chapter 5, how are you going to change your technique?

Before going on to Chapter 6, do you have a list of names, or sources of names, to call on when you begin your teleselling?

CHAPTER 6

The Attention-Grabber

The Key

> You have the first *20* seconds of a call in which to secure the undivided attention of your prospect. In order to be able to proceed beyond that time and achieve your call goal, you want to use that critical one-third of a minute to persuade your prospects that it is in their interest to talk with you. To best accomplish this, you should, after introducing yourself and your company, launch your conversation with an attention-grabbing statement that stresses one of your product's user-benefits. This chapter discusses why an attention-grabber is necessary and shows you how to create ones that will work for you.

The first challenge you face after getting your prospect on the telephone is to secure his or her attention for the duration of your call. While all salespeople face a similar challenge, it takes on increased importance in teleselling because your call is not planned for and is coming from a remote location, making it easier to cut you off.

Why an Attention-Grabber Is Necessary

The prospect will decide whether he or she wants to listen to you further as a result of the first 30 words you say. What you say, then, must be carefully thought out in advance.

Your task is further complicated by the fact that the prospect is likely to be occupied with something completely unrelated to your call when it comes through. Whether you are calling a consumer or a business person, your call creates the need for the prospect to shift gears mentally; your attention-grabber facilitates that process.

Also consider the advice, "First impressions count." Although prospects begin forming their impression of you the moment you say hello, the major impression begins forming as you start your introduction. What image do you want to create? How can you phrase and deliver an opening statement that fosters that image?

As teleselling catches on with a growing number of marketing organizations, there is also the increasing probability that you are not the only tele-seller to call the prospect on that day. What can you say that will set you apart from the others in the prospect's mind? How can you overcome the possible irritation a prospect feels as his work is interrupted once more by a teleseller? A strong, no-nonsense, attention-grabbing opening statement can go a long way toward marking you as a professional worth listening to.

Finally, you need to persuade the prospect to want to listen further to what you have to say. So among its other tasks, your attention-grabber will also have to sell for the time you need to carry out your full call strategy. A good opening will result in your having your prospect's undivided attention and will also stimulate an increased interest in your product. It may not only result in the realization of a need, but begin to create a desire to buy as well. And a strong, benefits-stressing opener can demonstrate your interest in your prospect and set the tone for the believability of the information you will be presenting.

You can achieve all of these effects with a preplanned, dramatic, interest-creating opening remark. In fact, you should work to develop several different opening remarks that start your sales calls in a smooth, professional manner. When you begin to work on the telephone, you will need several attention-grabbers. As you use and improve on them, others will come to mind. In the end, you want to have as many different ways to open your call as needed to get and hold your various prospects' attention.

Avoid ad libbing or "winging it." Even if you plan to use an extemporaneous delivery throughout your call, you will want to make an exception here. For your opener, you must plan what you are going to say, write it out, rehearse it, and deliver it *verbatim*. If you employ a script for your entire sales interview, this will just be the first of several planned and memorized sections of your call. And remember: Getting your prospect's attention turned exclusively to you is part of your effort to guide and direct the sales interview that begins the moment you say hello.

By planning your attention-grabbers carefully, and including a major prospect benefit in each one, you will get your calls off to a good start. When you have delivered an opening successfully, the prospect gives you close attention and wants to hear what else you have to say.

How to Get a Prospect's Undivided Attention

Attention-grabbing opening comments fall into several categories. First, you can open with a *general statement that sparks interest*. For example, you might say, "Mr. Wallace, I want to make you aware of how companies like yours have saved up to 50 percent of their meeting budget by making intelligent use of our teleconferencing network." Or: "Market Aids' slide charts are attractive, useful giveaways that have increased paid orders as much as 40 percent. I'm calling, Mr. Jacobi, to ask what your sales volume would be with a similar increase?" Develop several interest-creating general comments, being sure they are ones you are comfortable with and that reflect your personality and style.

Another way to attract attention is with *a sincere compliment.* "We are as proud of the durability of our jet spray nozzles as you are of your company's service. And our users report cutting down the amount of time their trucks are out of service for cleaning. I'm sure you want to achieve the same cost savings." Or, in acting on a referral, you might begin by acknowledging praise volunteered by the prospect with, "Thank you for passing on the nice things people at Ace Electronics had to say about us. I'm certain we can come up with a design that produces similar results for your company." The key word in this type of attention-grabber is "sincere." If you employ elaborate or false sincerity, you could offend your prospects, give the appearance of talking down to them, or otherwise damage the accuracy of your other selling statements.

You can also ask *key questions to get your prospect's attention.* An insurance teleseller, making an outgoing call to a mailed-in request for a premium quote, may see from the request that the prospect only has $5,000 in property damage coverage. She should begin the call by asking, "From the information you provided, I wondered what provisions you have made in the event you strike another car and it is a total loss?" and go on to point out, "At today's prices, 83 percent of all cars on the road are valued in excess of your $5,000 coverage." A textbook teleseller may ask a prospective user, "What are you going to do next semester now that the book you are using in class is out of print?"

A more difficult but equally effective technique is to make *the kind of startling statement that forces people to sit up and take notice.* To use an insurance example again, often employed by those selling homeowner policies, say, "Mr. Wynne, eight out of every ten people don't have enough coverage to replace their homes at present costs. If you are one of those eight, we can give you that protection, automatically, perhaps even at a lower premium than you are paying now."

You may want to open with *an analogy that captures your listener's interest.* From experience you know that your prospect faces problems similar to those of others with whom you have dealt. Relate those problems and your solutions directly to the prospect. You might say, "Mrs. Hipple, the Winkler Bakery in Jefferson City had rodents in their storage area. Our customized exterminating service solved that problem in three days, with techniques that protected the safety of the company's ingredients." After a pause, ask, "What do you do to combat vermin in your bakery?"

All of these techniques will grab attention. And with the appropriate opening, you are off to a good start in building a call that will conclude with a sale.

The early moments of your call are determined in part by conventional teleselling practices. Telephone courtesy demands that you first introduce yourself and your company. The next requirement, to state the purpose of the call, will be met by your attention-grabber. You can, in fact, employ a lead-in statement to make the transition from your introduction and attention-grabber to the body of your call by stating your purpose immediately. Some ways of doing this include:

1. A third-party reference: "I'm calling at the suggestion of our mutual acquaintance, Bill Johnson, who tells me you're looking for ways to cut the cost of your heating bills."

2. A follow-up to literature sent to the prospect: "I'm calling to follow up on the literature you requested to determine which of our marketing support functions can best produce the results you desire."

3. Reference to a recent advertisement or article you saw about the prospect or his company: "I read with interest about your experiments in increasing worker productivity. Handi-Mate, our stand-alone work station, reduces assembly time by making everything a worker needs available at one location, eliminating travel from one station to another for tools or parts."

4. Basing the opening on a known industry problem: "I'm calling to make you aware of our Push-Button Pilot, which eliminates the need for a continuously burning pilot light in your laundromat's dryers. You save money and conserve energy."

5. Relating your product to a point made by a prominent national or industry authority: "Mr. Jackson, Kenneth Roberts of the Harte Department Stores recently said that the key to increased sales is better merchandising or multiple options. Is that a marketing problem for your stores?" Go on to point out, "With our unique Retail-Plan Software you are able to plan, install, and track inventory turnover instantaneously, maximizing both the consumer's options and your profitability."

Some of the above examples introduce another key feature of your opener, the Initial Benefit Statement (IBS). It was pointed out earlier that the most effective attention-grabber includes a mention of the benefit to the prospect in buying your product. The IBS does that and a little more. It consists of three elements in one sentence: mention of the product by name, a statement of what's in it for the prospect, and proof in the form of features that deliver the benefit. Go back through the five examples given above. Separate out any initial benefit statements you can.

You'll find IBS's in #3: the Handi-Mate's increasing worker productivity by reducing assembly time. There's another in #4: Push-Button Pilot saves money and conserves energy by eliminating a continuous burning pilot light. And finally, look at #5: Retail Plan Software increases sales by maximizing customer options.

To create an IBS for your own selling, you will have to do some homework. What matters to the types of prospects you are going to call? The answer to that question can come from your prior experience with similar prospects. If you are entering new markets, read news and general articles or ads for related products to determine what is important to the person you'll be calling on. Another source of such information can be third-party referrals.

Your opening comments should be businesslike. Joking or frivolous comments could be interpreted as talking down to the prospect, or could indicate that you don't take what you are doing seriously. Be friendly and have confidence in yourself, but don't get cocky or mistake a prospect for a friend. Your positive attitude and conviction of the value of what you do should be apparent. Know and believe in your products, too.

Some telesellers apologize to the prospect for taking up their time, especially in their opening. Don't do it! An apology will be interpreted negatively, putting you on the defensive. Besides, there is no need to apologize if you believe in what you are doing. For your prospects to make intelligent buying choices and derive satisfaction and fulfillment from them, they need to be told the value of your products.

Finally, let your enthusiasm show from the very beginning. You have a lot to be enthusiastic about: You are offering a valuable product. You represent a first-class company. You are a well-trained professional teleseller. These facts should result in your being high on yourself, which will give you a tremendous psychological edge.

Use the examples presented here to start thinking about the types of things you are going to say to attract attention.

Creating Your Own Attention-Grabbers

Both telesellers who conduct their calls extemporaneously and those who work from a memorized or read script must write out, memorize, and rehearse their opening remarks. Developing and practicing a variety of these openers, so you can choose the best one for each prospect and situation, will get your calls off to a good start.

To begin creating effective openers for your selling situations, review the various categories of attention-grabbers on pages 54–55. Which of these (interest-creating, complimentary, or startling statements; key questions or analogies) is best suited to your personality and selling situation? Choose one or two to work with initially. But remember, one of the benefits of direct-response marketing is your ability to test the effectiveness of various techniques. Review your work regularly to see where you can make improvements.

Next, establish a profile of the prospects you will be talking with. What can you say to each of them that will get his or her attention? Look for guidance to their problems, concerns, needs, or desires. Research each situation and environment to provide insights. As you talk with a prospect, be alert for further signals. You learn as you go along.

Finally, examine your company's products. What benefits are suitable for you to use in your opening remarks? How will they vary from prospect to prospect? Again, test several statements to see which ones work best. The challenge is to come up with attention-grabbing statements that pack the most punch in the fewest words (remember, you have only 20 seconds). Chapter 13 has useful tips on word choice and use.

Now, write out as many attention-grabbing opening comments as you can, anywhere from three to twelve, to test and use on the telephone. Then go to the next page and check each for:

- your introduction
- mention of your company
- the purpose of your call
- an Initial Benefit Statement
- a maximum of 30 words

To review: Begin each call with a cheery "Hello!" Introduce yourself and your company. Then concentrate on getting the prospect's undivided attention with an effective attention-grabber. Generate interest in hearing what it is you have to say; snap your listener away from a preoccupation with other concerns. With your opening statement, set the tone for the whole call.

SELF INVENTORY   Yes   No

1. I plan what I am going to say before I get my prospect on the telephone.   ____   ____

2. My opening remark successfully grabs the prospect's attention.   ____   ____

3. I use various attention-grabbers, tailored to the product I am selling and the specific situation. ____   ____

4. My attention-grabbers include mention of at least one key product benefit.   ____   ____

5. I get the time I need to conduct the full call I planned.   ____   ____

For Thought and Action

How do you measure up on the performance goals of this chapter, as tested above?

Now that you've completed Chapter 6, how are you going to change your techniques?

Before you go on to Chapter 7, do you have a number of planned, memorized, attention-grabbing opening comments to use?

CHAPTER 7

Analyzing Needs

The Key

Before you can present your product as something that will satisfy a prospect's needs, you must know what those needs are. If you are using a previously written delivery, you call on your research and experience to help you draw up a profile of prospect needs, which your presentation will then show that the product can satisfy. If you plan extemporaneous presentations, you will use questions during the call to determine the prospect's specific needs and desires. In either case, you will close sales in proportion to how well you have analyzed a person's needs and sold product benefits to meet them. This chapter will increase your understanding of why needs analysis is so important to effective selling, and show you how to learn what you need to know to present your products in the best terms possible.

In analyzing a prospect's needs, what matters most are the things you must know in order to select the appropriate product from your line and present it in terms that satisfy those needs. To quickly and accurately determine those needs, ask questions and listen to all the prospect says. If you are selling only one product, the nature of your analysis changes, but not the analysis itself. You still want to learn which product features and benefits will excite each prospect individually. The more products you sell, or the more optional features your products have, the more you will *need* to analyze before you are able to present them in their best light.

Why Analyze Needs?

Now that you've gotten your prospect's attention and interest, what are you going to do with her? An inexperienced teleseller will think, "Aha! Now I'll sell her my product." Having reached this conclusion, he will jump right into a presentation and probably lose the sale. Why, then, does he do this? A beginner may be nervous and want to hide that fact by sounding authoritative. He will go to something he knows well: the product. Or he may be eager to succeed and think the only way to do that is to get in there and *sell*. But, as this teleseller gains experience, he will come to know the value of needs analysis. He will discipline himself to learn what his prospect wants before he tries to sell what he has. And if you, too, go to a sales presentation without analyzing what your prospect wants or needs, your chances of closing the sale are slim. Once you realize this, you won't think of skipping this step in your call strategy.

Analyzing a prospect situation to determine needs, or *qualifying*, actually began before you contacted the prospect. When you generated leads by matching call lists to product, you were identifying suspects by presumed needs. The process continued when you were cold-calling: You gave priority to all those suspects, thereby developing a list of prospects. If you sell to people who initiate the contact, a certain part of the initial analysis was done by them when they reached the decision to call you. Now that you have that prospect on the telephone and paying attention to you, you can analyze for the specific needs and desires your product can satisfy. Your job is to further refine, through questions and listening, whether this particular prospect is going to become a buyer. Is this prospect qualified to benefit from what you are selling? You must now establish, in your mind and theirs, what their needs are.

The analysis segment of your call strategy is another step in your systematically directing the conversation to a natural close. Go back to the model presented earlier. Remember, the single most important factor in your prospect's reaction to you is the interest you show in them, in their problems, needs, and concerns. You began to demonstrate that interest when you made your opening comment. Your needs analysis carries you even further into the confidence of the prospect. That is only one of the several important reasons to qualify a prospect before launching into a sales presentation. Some other reasons are:

1. Most important, this phase of the interview is intended as the place and way to determine how your products fit the prospect's needs and desires.
2. In those situations where you have a number of appropriate products, or your product has a number of optional features to tailor its usefulness, you will need to know more about the prospect and the prospect's situation before you can make a buying recommendation.
3. Questions that build interest in your product can create or increase a prospect's need or desire for your product.
4. Knowing what the prospect wants and needs enables you to build a sales presentation that creates a desire to buy.
5. The basics can quickly be determined. Are you talking to the decision-maker? If so, is that person in a position to buy at this time? Such things as budget cycles, the evaluation process, a group buying-decision process, can all influence whether or not you want to continue the call you are making.
6. In certain selling situations, you may have to determine whether a prospect can buy from you at all. For example, if you are the distributor of appliances to retail outlets, you cannot sell products to indi-

viduals who may contact you. Your agreement with your customers, the retail outlets, precludes that. Or your outbound teleblitz may inadvertently bring you into contact with a customer already buying from one of your company's territory-dedicated telesellers, or from an outside salesperson.

7. You will learn whether your prospect has the ability to pay. If the product cannot either be paid for outright or financed, there will be no sale. When you are selling large-scale items with high price tags, your marketing policy may include rigid financial guidelines for you to follow. Consumer telesellers often have to determine family income levels or cash availability before they can proceed to close a sale. In either case, you have to learn from your records and from the prospect whether he or she can afford your product. If not, it is time for a polite good-bye, and on to the next prospect.

8. The information you gain can help you anticipate and thus minimize the number and intensity of the objections that will arise.

9. You will implant in the mind of the prospect the idea that you are indeed an expert, since you know what to ask and how to get at what really matters. The prospect's confidence in you will grow accordingly.

10. Your professional integrity is enhanced in the prospect's eyes when you make the right product recommendation.

Beyond your ability to analyze needs, you want to be able to create desires to buy that did not exist prior to your call. Desires differ from needs primarily in the perception of the prospect. Develop *questions* to ask during your analysis that will create the need or the desire to buy. The following are examples of questions intended to create desires:

1. How much could you save in a year, Mr. Brandt, if we cut 30 percent off your home heating bill each month?

2. Would you sleep easier knowing Master-Guard windows were impossible to penetrate from the outside?

3. How would you use the three extra hours a week you'd save with our home pickup and delivery laundry service?

Because desires grow from emotional bases—the absence of a real need is outweighed by an impulse to have—this last activity is more characteristic of consumer teleselling than of business-to-business sales. But don't sell the role of emotion short in *all* buying decisions. A review of the buying motives in Chapter 2 should persuade you anew of how important emotion and perceived need are in reaching a buying decision. The questions above and similar ones will help you prepare your prospect for a favorable buying decision at the end of the call.

You may encounter people who are impatient with the analysis process. When you do, and you feel they are qualified to buy, point out how a thorough analysis will benefit them: First, it will help them to clarify their thinking and give priority to their own needs. By filling you in completely, they ensure that you will recommend only the most appropriate product, options, or configurations, those that are best suited to their needs. And this saves time as well, both during the call itself and later, by minimizing the chance of their receiving a product that doesn't do what is needed or wanted.

Recall from earlier presentations that in selling, the odds are overwhelmingly against you. If you were to work at random, you would close 1 sale in 450 calls. Throughout your work, you strive to better those odds. And needs analysis is an integral part of such a strategy. When properly employed, it will increase your chances of closing a sale. Keeping that in mind, don't short-cut the analysis of your prospect's needs.

How to Analyze Needs

If you have been following the procedures advocated here, you already know a little about your prospect. Qualifying began before you initiated contact, and continues in the earliest phases of your call. Such factors as why you contact whom you do, your company's marketing strategy, and the profile of existing customers have drawn parameters around a segment of the universe at large. Your prospects could be targeted by age, by geographic location, by income level, sex, or home, car, stereo or TV ownership, to name a few characteristics. Industrial tellsellers could concentrate on geographic territories, type of industry (those SIC #'s), or level of business size, sales, or sophistication.

This pre-screening activity, therefore, has been done and is not the qualifying you're concerned with in your on-the-telephone interview. Either those factors are now beyond your control or the needed influences have already worked. You now want to prepare your strategy for when you have the desired prospect on the telephone.

But there is no substitute for your person-to-person exchange with the prospect as the backbone of your needs analysis. The subsequent form of all other steps in the call strategy depend on it. It is here that the sales call comes to life. Like a gold prospector, you are panning to gather in the nuggets you know are there. You will interact with the prospect, demonstrating your interest in his or her problems and concerns. You are setting the stage for providing information that points out the proven benefits of what you are selling, information that will enable you to close the sale.

First, before you create your strategy, review the objective of your call. Call objectives for a one-call-to-close are different from those in a planned three-calls-to-close campaign. Other factors affecting your objectives are your product and market. If you are selling consumer goods, you will probably place more emphasis on creating a need or desire to buy than you would in selling industrial goods. It may be a more "emotional" sale, perhaps of a product that doesn't fill any basic need. The same problem faces those business-to-business tellsellers who work with such intangibles as training programs, consulting services, or word-processing software. In either case, you may have to create a need or desire to buy that is not initially apparent to the prospect.

To analyze and determine needs to fill before you get on the telephone, consider the data you may already have on the prospect. If the individual wrote you, look at the information that was provided, with an eye to screening out inappropriate products. Also look for information gaps that you will need to fill in during the call. Don't assume anything, or generalize about missing data. You want to show prospects that you have their needs, concerns, and interests at heart. You can't do that if you jump to conclusions before contacting them.

Before launching into the analysis, it may prove useful to know what factors will knock a prospect out of consideration and back into the universe as an unqualified prospect. Some of these "knock-out" factors may help prevent spending wasted time with a person on the telephone. Depending on the marketing context of your call, the knock-out factors can vary from short but specific (for cold-call teleblitzing to generate leads) to long but general (to better determine what specific products to present and close on). Such factors as "must be a homeowner," "has pre-school-age children," or "present insurance expires within 60 days" can screen a consumer in or out. In the business-to-business market, credit rating, volume of sales, specific business activity, and the potential size of the order may be among dictated knock-out factors. List here those factors in your marketing guidelines that disqualify potential buyers:

1. _____
2. _____
3. _____
4. _____
5. _____

Now that you are ready to begin qualifying a prospect, there are four ways to do it: (a) using *data available on company forms, or using those forms as a guide*; (b) *asking open-ended questions*; (c) *asking closed questions*; and (d) *listening effectively*. You can use these individually or in any combination to get what you need to present your product and close the sale.

First there is the data that you have gathered through established channels: application forms, orders, requests for information. They are a good source of guidance to you in determining what makes a qualified prospect. Look for the specific information you will need to gather. Look at the forms you will be using (or designing). What do they tell you? List below the ways in which these forms can assist you in your analysis:

1. _____
2. _____
3. _____
4. _____
5. _____

After you have reviewed this information, more elaborate data-gathering, as needed, can be done by asking questions. The kinds of questions you ask will fall into two categories.

First, there are open-ended questions, intended to induce the prospect to give a full, expository answer—not just a yes, no, or other short response. They draw the prospect out for a discussion of their needs, problems, and concerns. Use open-ended questions when you want a lot of information of a general nature: "What factors are important to you in selecting lists of prospects for your telemarketing operation?" is one such operation. The information you gather using this type of question can then be used to pose additional questions. For example, you might follow the initial question with, "You say you look for prospects who bought a related product recently; are there any criteria about the purchase that are important to further screening?"

Open questions begin with such words as "what," "when," "how," "where," and "which." They are all intended to get prospects to discuss their situation with you. And while the prospect is talking, you are noting needs, clues to buying motives, concerns, and opportunities to stress a benefit. If your strategy calls on you to gather a lot of information during the analysis/qualifying phase of your call, open questions are best suited to your need.

Think about your qualifying situations and write out below some of the *open-ended* questions you are apt to pose during a call:

1. _____
2. _____
3. _____
4. _____
5. _____

The second type of question you can ask is the closed question. These questions are direct, and call for a one-word, or short, answer; "yes", "no", or "not over $4,500." "Do you have room on your shelves to take advantage of our quantity discount, Mrs. Wafer?" is such a question. The advantages of the closed question include being able to get through data collection rapidly, and filling in gaps left by answers to open-ended questions. They also help bring a talkative prospect, the kind who seems to go on forever, under control. Finally, your open questions may have uncovered some unanticipated needs that you want a little more data on so as to prepare your sales message and stress appropriate benefits.

Think again about the qualifying you will do and list some of the *closed* questions you will need to ask. You can use such words as "do," "has," "can," "will," and "should" to begin closed questions.

1. _____
2. _____
3. _____
4. _____
5. _____

With practice, you can begin to make the ultimate use of closed questions: phrasing them in such a way that the other party *has* to answer yes. They get in the habit of agreeing with you. That can be indispensable when you get to the close and they find they have to agree with you once again, acknowledging that your product meets their needs. Although clearly most suited to simple, one-call-close situations, it is a valid technique for you as you plan what you are going to ask while analyzing a prospect's needs.

In addition to gathering information, the questioning technique gets the prospect to interact with you and participate in the sale. That builds interest in your product and confidence in you, both of which are essential in the successful selling situation. And, prospects' answers will provide you with insights into their thinking and their likely reaction to your upcoming presentation.

The answers you get to the questions you ask help you diagnose needs. It is your responsibility to develop your own list of needs-analysis questions for each product you represent and each prospect situation you encounter. Once you have the information these questions elicit, you are in a position to develop an effective action-getting presentation.

The final key to analysis is to listen to all a prospect is saying, since they will probably tell you things about themselves and their situation that further clarify your understanding of their needs, concerns, and desires. Listening closely and interpreting the answers help determine what benefits to stress in your selling message. Just as important, you will need to listen for buying motives, the factors that will influence the buying decision. These opportunities may not arise in the course of formal questioning.

Use the data you gather to plan the order in which you will stress the benefits of your product. Determine what is most important to the prospect, and plan to immediately and continually reinforce the information on how your product meets those needs. What factors are less important? They will have to be dealt with in your presentation, but with less emphasis. And what things are not important? To someone with a robot assembly line, the improved worker morale your machine fosters would be of little interest. Skip it! . . . and everything else about your product that doesn't address specific needs of individual prospects.

Finally, listen to learn more about your market and your competitors. Suppose, for example, you want to set up a presentation of your superior customer service. You might ask, "How are your orders handled by your present supplier?" The answer you get may not only give you insight into how important customer service is to the prospect, but also information about your competition. And it may uncover some heretofore unknown problem your product or company can solve.

Listening, therefore, becomes as important a skill as phrasing the proper questions. Don't ask good questions, and then miss the full answers. By listening to *all* a prospect has to say, whether in answer to your questions or in casual conversation, you will be able to pick up additional hints and information on what the prospect will be looking for in making a buying decision. Listen closely, and hear not just the words being spoken, but the hidden meanings they may carry as well.

In conclusion, the art of asking questions to elicit needed responses is a technique used by every successful teleseller. This is not the idle kind of questioning that accompanies friendly conversation (although that is the effect you are trying to create); sales-directed questioning requires both planning and thought in order to be effective. You are trying to guide and direct this conversation to your preset goal: a closed sale. The answers you get to your questions help you to diagnose your prospect's needs. They provide data and give you insights you will need in assembling and delivering your presentation and in asking for the order.

SELF INVENTORY   Yes   No

1. I think of myself as a problem solver.   ____   ____
2. I gather the prospect information I need before
making my sales presentation.   ____   ____
3. I ask questions to determine my prospect's needs
and wants.   ____   ____
4. My analysis is intended to also create a need or
desire to buy.   ____   ____
5. I empathize with my prospect as I conduct my
analysis.   ____   ____

For Thought and Action

How do you measure up on the performance goals of this chapter, as tested above?

Now that you've completed Chapter 7, how are you going to change your analysis techniques?

Before going on to Chapter 8, have you prepared a set of both open-ended and closed questions you can ask your prospects to determine their needs?

CHAPTER 8

An Action-Getting Presentation

The Key

> You want to present the product you've chosen—the one that best
> fills the prospect's needs or meets his or her desires—in a way that
> gets sales action. You must learn to methodically build your pre-
> sentation around benefits that show the prospect your product does
> what is needed and wanted. This applies whether your calls are
> scripted or not. If the call is going to lead to a sale, there must be
> no doubt in the prospect's mind that your product is desirable and
> will deliver what is promised. This chapter considers the relative
> merits of scripted and extemporaneous deliveries for this phase of
> your call, and then shows you what goes into a sales-getting pre-
> sentation, regardless of which you use, and how to develop pre-
> sentations for use in selling your own products.

You now have a call objective and a strategy to help you achieve it. You
have gotten your prospect's attention and, through questioning and attentive
listening, analyzed what the person's needs are. You are ready to present the
product you'd recommend in a manner that gets sales action. In order to do
that, you want to be prepared for any eventuality. By developing broad outlines for presentations that cover most situations you are likely to encounter,
you will be in a position to give a well-thought-out presentation that does not
come across as a canned pitch.

Scripted Versus Extemporaneous Delivery

A long-running debate in telephone selling concerns the importance and
value of scripted selling messages over planned but extemporaneous ones.
Nowhere are the implications of this debate felt more heavily than during the
actual presentation of your product. Earlier you were urged to make a script
of your opening statement. That is important in order to get all of the elements of an introduction, including at least one attention-grabbing Initial
Benefit Statement, before your prospect in just twenty seconds. A script that
is carefully planned, rehearsed, and delivered word for word is crucial to your
opening.

People who favor a script for the entire presentation point out the following advantages:

1. Anyone can deliver a script. With a minimum of training and start-up time, additional tellsellers can be hired, or scripts that have been tested and proven can be farmed out to a service company.
2. There is better control over the quality of the call. If you are working with other tellsellers, you can be sure each of you is delivering the same presentation, making the same offer, and asking for the order—all in a way known to be successful.
3. You won't forget something important. In handling a large volume of calls and interacting with many different prospects, possibly even under pressure, it is normal that key features are sometimes skipped during the presentation. Scripting avoids this possibility.
4. A script ensures effective time management. If you expect to complete a set number of calls per hour, the script removes the temptation to digress, initiate small talk, or otherwise drift into conversations that take longer than planned.
5. You can measure the variables in your presentation more easily. By making changes in the script that affect how such things as key benefits and the price offer are presented, and keeping accurate records of the results, you can determine almost immediately what works best—if benefit A induces more favorable responses than benefit B, or stressing a discount gets better results than a low base price.
6. You exercise maximum control over the course of the call. You initiate questions where *you* want or need them, head off objections, and phrase benefits for maximum effect, allowing you to better direct the call to your desired result.
7. A script can increase your confidence in yourself, putting your mind at ease if you are uncertain of your skills. This is especially important for someone new to teleselling.

But scripted delivery has its disadvantages, too. You will want to consider them before you make up your presentation. They include:

1. A scripted message can come out sounding like the canned pitch it is—especially after numerous deliveries, when it becomes second nature.
2. The prospect you are calling may not really fit your script, which may miss the mark completely and address benefits that are not important to that individual. This will be immediately obvious to the prospect, and the teleseller will get tuned out.
3. Today's sophisticated buyer may see the script for what it indeed is: an attempt to fit the prospect to the teleseller's needs rather than the other way around.
4. The teleseller's credibility as a problem-solver, interested in the prospect's needs and concerns, may be undermined.
5. If the script misses the mark and unanticipated questions arise, you

may be in a jam. A script inhibits creative, free-thinking responsiveness on the part of the teleseller.

6. A canned pitch may be viewed by many prospects as condescending. And you may appear artificial and insincere, as if you have a low opinion of the intelligence and creativity of the prospect.

7. The script may pack too much into the presentation: too many benefits, an overwhelming array of data, even answers to common objections that the prospect wouldn't have thought of if you hadn't brought them up.

8. A script is inflexible and can lead you to be that way yourself. Say you want to buy a scripted teleseller's product in the middle of the message and listen to the shuffling of pages as he struggles to find out what he is to say next.

In response to these shortcomings, many tellsellers are increasingly using a loosely planned, segmented selling presentation. It may include some memorization, such as of five key product benefits or the three most common product applications in specific situations. But the action-getting presentation itself is delivered extemporaneously, taking into consideration such factors as the prospect's needs, desires, personality type, and decision-making process.

In addition to overcoming some of the shortcomings of the scripted message mentioned here, an extemporaneous delivery can:

- demonstrate your interest in the prospect
- enable you to tailor each call to exact prospect needs
- make it easier for you to adapt to marketing changes without having to retrain or write everything out before getting on the telephone

The principles presented below will enable you to create scripted presentations. The decision whether or not to script your presentation should be made only after weighing the pros and cons mentioned and applying each to your own marketing and call strategies. However, as a trained, professional, situation-responsive teleseller, you will probably most often encounter situations that would make scripted presentations either inappropriate or offensive. In anticipation of these, you should develop the ability to create flexible, planned sales messages that are delivered extemporaneously; action-getting messages that lead to the prospect's wanting to buy.

The Elements of a Planned Presentation

You know that the most important factor in prospects' reactions to you is your interest in their needs and concerns. The part of your call that best demonstrates that interest is the action-getting presentation. This is your opportunity—building on the rapport, integrity, and believability you've developed thus far in the interview—to show your interest in and understanding of the prospect by presenting your recommended product in terms of his or her needs.

Planning is essential for an action-getting sales presentation. Planning what you will say lets you have more influence over the course of the call. It ensures that you cover all the points important to a prospect. Planning will give you the confidence needed to overcome nervousness and eliminate poor speech mannerisms. And with planning you will have maximum impact on the call's outcome: the achievement of your selling goal.

With the volume of calls you handle, you don't have time to carefully plan out and rehearse each sales message individually. Nor do you need to. Most of your presentations will be similar, and it is neither necessary nor appropriate to think up new messages and strategies each time you handle a call. You don't read your operator's manual each time you get into your car. Similarly, the way in which you stress a benefit, guide the conversation, and secure buyer agreement is suitable for use in most teleselling situations. By planning in advance, you can respond to the vast majority of the situations that arise in the calls you handle.

Finally, knowing in advance the broad outlines of what you are going to say will give you the freedom to listen for that unique combination of prospect needs that each selling opportunity presents. You can be creative in building your presentation in a short period of time, using the elements from your pre-planned sales message that you deem appropriate.

There is a natural break in the call-flow pattern as you wrap up your analysis of needs. You have been gathering data, singling out specific needs, refining your understanding of the situation. You will know, and your prospect will sense, when you have gathered the information you need and are ready to move from the analysis to a presentation. You have reached that point when your training, experience, and intuition tell you that you can confidently select the one product that gives the best chance of closing the sale.

The action-getting presentation phase of your call can follow a basic format that broadly applies to each sales-message outline you develop. This leaves you free to plug in appropriate statements stressing benefits specific to the particular prospect. It is, in fact, a microsales presentation, consisting of:

- an attention-getting opening statement
- the transition statement carrying your prospect from the general opener to specifics relevant to him or her
- the body of the presentation

Your goal, then, is to have planned teleselling messages, brief outlines of what you will say, arranged in a tentative order, for each major segment of the presentation. And remember, you want to build those segments around benefits to the prospect. For example, you will have an outline for effectively presenting the "guaranteed lifetime renewal protection" feature of your automobile insurance policies as a benefit your analysis showed to be important to the prospect. It will consist of the three steps mentioned. You should make a similar outline for each product benefit you identify. Either all of them together or a select number of them will form your action-getting presentation.

There are a number of reasons (in the form of benefits) why the prospect should want to buy your product. While certain benefits may be available from competitors, and all are usually available individually elsewhere, your particular combination is what makes you unique. And it gives you a strong marketing message to deliver. You want to tell your prospect the company's story, and to stress the unique opportunity of doing business with the only source in the marketplace for this combination. Below, list as many benefits as you can think of which, when added up, equal the unique product available only through you and your company. Note how you might phrase these benefits in such a way as to use them in your attention-getting presentation.

1. _____
2. _____
3. _____
4. _____
5. _____

This list adds up to the compelling reason your product is desirable. Did you remember to include yourself as one of the benefits your company offers? If not, you'll want to pay particular attention to Chapter 12.

This combination of benefits you have listed is what makes your offering unique. The combined package is available only from you, regardless of the price.

Developing an Action-Getting Presentation

In teleselling, having a well-thought-out plan for each segment of your presentation enables you to tell your story in a spontaneous, natural, enthusiastic manner in the time allowed.

Your first objective in the presentation is to renew the prospect's attention to the purpose of your call. That may have become obscured as you worked through your analysis. As with your initial attention-grabber, your goal is to arouse interest and create a desire to hear more. It takes forethought and effort to make effective attention-getting comments. And there are a number of ways to do it.

You can begin by asking a series of questions. Each question serves to get, build, and keep the prospect's attention. A teleseller of office supplies may do this by asking (after determining that cost-savings is a need of the prospect), "How many dollars would you save if I can arrange a Constant Customer Credit account that reduces your costs by as much as 23 percent?" A person selling home improvements to a consumer who said convenience was a key need might ask, "Would you invest in a total home security system that can be initiated from your bedside, which you can install yourself with only a screwdriver, all at a price that's competitive with other, less sophisticated systems?"

Employed another way, questions can serve you by summarizing needs. The insurance teleseller does this by beginning her presentation: "Do I understand correctly that you want coverage that offers adequate protection in a high inflation economy, that has convenient claim service, and that carries lifetime renewal protection? Is that right, Mr. Roper?" This kind of questioning confirms your understanding of the prospect's needs and desires. You are getting the prospect to participate in your presentation by answering yes, the beginning of an oral contract between you and the prospect to share in the outcome of the call. And you are ensuring that the other party will want to listen with interest to what you are about to say.

Another way to initiate your presentation is to tell about the experience of a customer whose needs or situation is similar to that of your prospect. Your laundry home pickup and delivery service has saved many of the prospect's neighbors, people just like her, time and money. (Mention names here, if you have your customers' permission to do so. If not, get that permission.) The situation referred to should clearly be relevant to that prospect, and its conclusion should be pertinent to the points you plan in your presentation and close. Success stories can be especially powerful. A textbook teleseller can generate interest and excitement by opening her presentation with a statement describing how another school district's use of her basic-reading-text package resulted in a rise in reading scores and retention rates. Show the prospect how you and your company helped someone with similar needs, which you were able to satisfy.

Well-told stories, when carefully chosen and free from controversy, can, in the opening part of your presentation, build interest and secure agreement (spoken as well as unspoken) on the part of the prospect.

Making a dramatic or challenging statement is another technique that starts presentations off with impact. For instance, you might use a statistical analysis, such as, "One out of every two Americans does not have enough coverage to protect himself from personal financial loss in the event of an accident." Or you could set up a hypothetical case you know to exist among companies like the one your prospect represents: "Firms such as yours have lost an average of $3.5 million a year by using security services that do not bond their guards." If you are going to start with a dramatic statement, make it appropriate to the prospect's needs, as determined by your analysis.

As an exercise, choose two or three prospect needs and/or buying motives you encounter (or are likely to) most frequently. For each, choose an attention-getting technique and write out what you would say to begin your sales presentation to that need or those buying motives.

The presentation starter is a short moment in the call, usually no more than one or two brief sentences. Next you need a short transition statement, one that will aid you in going from the general tone of your opening statement to the specifics you will have to speak in to close the sale or otherwise get the prospect's agreement.

This passage from attention-getting to presentation of product can again be done with questions, stories, or dramatic statements. If you employed a question-asking technique for opening your presentation, you could make your transition by finally asking, "Now, why are these questions important for you to think about when considering our product?" Or you could explain why the statistical statement you made came to mind while you were talking to this prospect: "Our review of your orders with us in the past six months indicates you may soon be facing that problem unless you upgrade your account now." Finally, use a dramatic statement when appropriate: "Based on what you have told me, Mr. Moore, you will save over $75 a month in fuels costs alone with the newest furnace in our line."

Stop here and build transition statements suitable for use with the attention-getting opening strategies you developed a few minutes ago.

1. _____
_____
2. _____
_____
3. _____
_____

You are at the point now where you are ready to recommend your product for the prospect's consideration. If you have more than one product that fits the prospect's needs, your analysis of needs has told you which one to recommend. If you have only one product for the situation, you will have to choose the most beneficial features of the product for this particular prospect. In either case, everything you have been doing up to this point has been in preparation for what you are about to do and say now. Your action-getting presentation has reached the point at which you can pull together all your skills as a teleselling professional: your communication techniques, product knowledge, and persuasive selling skills, which are enhanced by your enthusiasm and empathy.

You should, as your conversation with the prospect develops, be thinking of how what is being said will fit into and affect your presentation. In that way, when the body of your presentation is before you, you are not pulling ideas out of a hat. Rather, you are moving into a planned portion of the call that you will have assembled as your needs analysis unfolded. Your presentation will:

- include a point-by-point coverage of the needs of the prospect
- stress product benefits to the prospect, telling what's in the purchase for him or her
- feature an orientation that emphasizes and demonstrates the fulfillment of the prospect's needs

Begin by quickly ordering, in your mind, the most important needs, desires, and concerns of your prospect. If you sense the prospect has a ranking of their order of importance, follow it.

Second in your list are those requirements that, while important, are not the most pressing. These you will address or minimize.

Finally, using a combination of your intuition and experience, set aside discussion of benefits you feel are not important or which may have been false leads.

Equipped with such a ranked list in your mind, you now want to move through it, addressing each point in a way that stresses the benefit to the prospect of buying your product. Review Chapter 3 to refresh yourself on selling product features and advantages as benefits.

Enthusiasm, word choice, pacing, and voice inflection all will help you deliver an interesting, forceful message. Keep your talk in sequence, hitting most often the benefits that are most important to the prospect. Bring up other, less important benefits as the opportunity arises. As you gain experience, you will find it increasingly easier to hammer home an effective, enthusiastic, action-getting presentation.

But don't get carried away. Too many high points or too many benefits may confuse your prospect. You don't want to go over a shopping list of every possible benefit you can think of. Limit yourself to the top two or three in the mind of the prospect, and sell them well. Remember, you are building your message to that final step: asking for an order.

As you cover each benefit, conclude your presentation by showing how it relates directly to the prospect. "Can you see, Mr. Moore, where you can save $75 a month on heating bills?" "Does the six-hour fulfillment that our automated process guarantees, with toll-free access for you, satisfy your requirement, Mrs. Craig?" Secure agreement and move on to your next benefit, or handle any objections you encounter (this is discussed in detail in the next chapter).

Your action-getting presentation comes and goes very quickly. It begins with its own attention-getter. Then you make a transition to the body of your talk, carrying the prospect from the general to his or her specific situation. Finally, if the prospect voices no objections, as a natural conclusion to the conversation you must proceed directly to step 5 and ask for the order. That's it. If you are well-prepared, enthusiastic, and empathetic, this will be one of the more rewarding parts of your work. It is just plain exciting to present the right product to the right person in a manner that gets a sale.

SELF INVENTORY   Yes   No

1. I have planned selling presentations I can tailor
to different circumstances as the need arises.   ____   ____
2. My action-getting presentation is both system-
atic and logical.   ____   ____
3. I describe my product in terms that demonstrate
its benefits to the prospect.   ____   ____
4. My action-getting presentation creates a need
and a desire to buy my product.   ____   ____
5. My presentation reflects what I learned during
my analysis of needs.   ____   ____

For Thought and Action

How do you measure up on the performance goals of this chapter, as tested above?

Now that you've completed Chapter 8, how are you going to change your sales-presentation techniques?

Before going on to Chapter 9, have you developed presentation outlines for the major products you will be selling on the telephone?

Answering Objections

The Key

Prospects can at any time object to buying your product. If they didn't, your work wouldn't be very challenging. This chapter will help you develop techniques to respond to each type of objection likely to arise in your day-to-day teleselling and overcome them. It will show you how to set up an Objection Handbook to assist you in being on top of most objections you will encounter.

If you have essentially completed the presentation stage of the call, you and your prospect have been cooperating. You have been guiding and directing the conversation, and have created in the prospect an assumption of a mutual interest: your product and his or her need for it. But when it comes time to ask for the order, you are likely to begin encountering a defensive strategy, one based on objections. Objections are those obstacles, either real or imagined, that stand between you and a closed sale. Learning how to overcome or answer objections and go on to close a sale is a skill fundamental to all teleselling.

The Challenge of Objections

The only salesperson who won't encounter an objection is one who is the sole representative of a product that everyone needs to survive. Since that does not describe you, the first realization for you to come to is this: Objections are going to arise. Knowing this, you can get on with the real challenge: answering them and going on to close the sale.

When are you likely to encounter objections? If you include the screen that you must get through as an objection, expect them immediately. And they can occur at any other time during the course of the call as well. The prospect who interrupts your attention-grabber with "I'm too busy now, call me next month!" has hit you with an objection. Other early objections include, "Send me some literature on your product and I'll get back to you," and "I'm not the right person to talk to." You must be ready for objections as soon as you get a prospect on the line.

However, the call flow presented here anticipates that the most likely place for objections to arise is either during the action-getting presentation or when you have completed it and ask for the order. It is at the latter time that your prospect has to decide whether to buy or not. Faced with such a decision, your listener will probably begin thinking of the reasons not to buy. As these reasons come to mind, the prospect will present them to you as obstacles preventing him or her from buying now—or ever.

Remember, though, this is not always the case. One of the most gratifying moments in selling comes when you have wrapped up your presentation and asked your prospect to buy, and the answer is yes, without hesitation. It happens more frequently than you may think. On average, with a "soft" offer ("Send it back if you aren't satisfied, we'll refund your money and pay the postage.") you can expect a favorable reaction about two or three times an hour from a qualified list. With a hard offer, where the decision is thought to be final (although it never really is until the invoice is paid), one close an hour is a job well done. People do have needs, want products to satisfy them, and buy when so persuaded. As one sales trainer put it, "Sales usually aren't lost. They go to the competition."

Going back to objections, there are a number of reasons why they arise:

1. Some people are simply not open to change or are unwilling to take risks. If your attention-grabber and analysis of needs (assuming you got this far with these people) didn't persuade them otherwise, get off the telephone. Experience and empathy will enable you to spot such a prospect, even if it is someone who has participated politely in your call. Once you detect rigidity, disengage.
2. Some people simply object out of habit. For them, saying no is second nature, perhaps developed as a first line of defense against buying anything.
3. Hard as you may find it to believe, some objections arise because of your mistakes. You may not have properly qualified the prospect and have therefore presented the wrong product. You may have been misunderstood because you were unclear in your explanation of how the product meets the needs, or nebulous about how the prospect will benefit.
4. Nor is the prospect without an occasional shortcoming. He or she may be sincerely interested but vague and evasive in describing needs, making it difficult for you to make a strong presentation. The resulting objections are usually easy to handle, though.
5. Objections can result from the fact that you have not created a sufficient need or desire to buy in the mind of the prospect. He may want to be further convinced that your product will do what you say. He will compare what you have said with what he knows of other, competing, products; he wants to get the best product at the best price.
6. Most objections result from legitimate concern on the part of prospects: They want a full picutre of what they are buying and how it suits their needs.

Objections take different forms, but they mostly fall into four distinct categories:

The stall. This may be difficult to detect and deal with because it doesn't sound like an objection at all. In fact, it can sound downright positive, and make much sense. "Yes, I'm interested. Send me some literature." "We will be deciding that next month, call me back then." "I have to consult my wife before we make a decision like that. Can we call you back?" Examine statements such as these, which you will hear regularly. Which of them could be just putting you off?

The misunderstanding. This objection is obvious, easily recognized when it arises. The prospect merely didn't understand what you said, or misinterpreted it. "But I don't need one right now [which may also mean, 'I can't afford it now.']. And it will be sold by the time I do," is such a case, and a golden opportunity to stress a new benefit: your layaway or interest-free deferred-payment plan. The problem you face here is similar to that of a major league second baseman going after an easy ground ball: Easy as it may seem, if he doesn't do it right, he'll be charged with an error and the batter will be safe. The misunderstanding has to be handled, as do all other objections. What misunderstandings arise after your presentations? If some occur frequently, rework your benefits outlines in an attempt to prevent them.

The false objection. You know from experience or from your records that this just isn't so. The prospect who says he doesn't need to make a buying decision soon, when you know his existing supply of a product is about to run out, has raised a false objection. When you are sure the objection is false, it may be a warning to you that this prospect is a lost cause. If a prospect continually raises false objections, consider terminating the call and moving on to other, more interested prospects.

The real objection. Since they are based on facts, such objections must be dealt with, answered, and closed. They result from the prospect's analysis of their situation and experience in light of what you are presenting. The objection could be to price—perhaps your product really does cost more than a similar product from a competitor. Or it could be based on the fact that your product lacks some feature or combination of features that is important to the prospect. Real objections must be dealt with in a direct, no-nonsense manner, and you will learn how to do so later in this chapter.

As you have seen from the examples above, objections can take the form of either questions or declarative statements. And you must be especially sensitive to statements that sound innocuous but are in fact objections.

Before turning to specific techniques for handling objections, consider a couple of ways of initially heading them off. First, with a little planning, and a sensitivity to what you will or have encountered on the telephone, you can avoid some of the most frequent or serious objections likely to arise. You can do this with a technique called *the preemptive statement*: You answer the objection before it is voiced.

Consider, for example, that you notice you are getting an increasing number of complaints that your replacement supplies have been very slow to arrive. The result is that existing customers have been going to a competitor for supplies, and, because of your reputation for slow fulfillment (spread by word of mouth), you are experiencing difficulty in getting new customers as well. Assuming you have done something to correct this serious business deficiency, you can now head off the objection that you know will be forthcoming. In this instance, your preemptive statement may occur near the end of your presentation: "Our new, automated fulfillment center, with a 24-hour toll-free number, gives you the assurance that we will ship your order within six hours of receiving it. This new system is state-of-the-art, and has not only won recognition in our industry, but has received acclaim from our customers as well." Go on to close the objection with, "If you like, I can send you several recent letters from satisfied customers, testifying to what I am saying." This preemptive statement could also be the reason for your call to past customers, and it could appear as early as your attention-getter when you are calling these people.

In any case, you have defused a major objection. Keep track of your most frequently encountered objections—ones you know can be handled. Develop similar preemptive statements to integrate appropriately into your planned call, and begin deflecting those objections.

One cautionary note—especially relevant to planning your preemptive strategy but applicable throughout your call—concerns that dreaded mental exercise, jumping to conclusions. If you hear particular objections on occasion and they are ones you know not to be based on your product or company's deficiency, you may conclude that everyone you talk with is going to raise these objections. Such a prejudice on your part is dangerous to your sales health. You will, in a defensive mood, either bring up the objection or answer it when the prospect has not thought to make it, and you will have effectively planted in the prospect's mind another reason not to buy. Handling objections that are brought up will keep you busy enough; don't add to your difficulties.

Some objections arise when you least expect them. You want to be ready to deflect these smoothly until an appropriate time in your planned call. This can frequently be done with a comment like, "You've raised an important question, Mrs. Walker. In a moment I will walk you through our order-processing procedure and you will see why you can have every confidence that your order will be in your hands no more than two days after you place it— even earlier at only a slight extra charge if you need air freight service." If you cannot control the conversation to delay objections, you should handle them when they arise, either by jumping to your preemptive statement or by asking the prospect to hold off a few moments. If you employ the latter technique, make a written note of the objection and be sure you come back to it as promised.

There is nothing wrong with being stumped by an objection the first time you encounter it. This happens repeatedly, even to the best sales people, despite thorough preparation. It is, however, inexcusable to be stopped by that same objection a second time. It means you weren't responsive the first time it arose, and didn't give it a second thought. To prevent that from happening to you, you should begin an Objection Handbook. This is a place for you to write down the key data concerning each objection, think it through, and prepare an answer to it. The form below can be reproduced either on pages for a looseleaf notebook or on 5-by-8 notecards, for use in establishing your Objection Handbook.

Product:
Objection Encountered:
Where in the Call It Most Frequently Occurs:
Possible Motivations:
Answers:
Balance-Sheet Reply:

Note: See page 83 for an explanation of balance-sheet replies.

When you meet an objection that you fail to handle to your complete satisfaction, write it down as soon as you get off the telephone. Then give thought as to what might motivate such an objection: impatience, misunderstanding, an inappropriate buying motive you hadn't anticipated, a real concern for the correctness of what you are saying, or some other factor. Think how you might answer it if it arises again. Consult others to see if they have encountered it and, if so, how they handled it. Also check your product literature to learn benefits you can use to overcome the objection. Finally, formulate a strategy, using the techniques described in the next section of this chapter, to handle it the next time it arises. What *exactly* will you say? Have the answers outlined and within reach at all times, or committed to memory.

Adopt the attitude that every objection has an answer. You should be prepared to handle the objections you are likely to hear. By using your Objection Handbook regularly, in a very short time you will have noted and planned a response to almost all the objections you will encounter.

Some examples of common objections, taken from situations that occur during the screening out of nonqualified prospects, illustrate this point. The prospect may say she has just bought your product or one just like it. She may have a large inventory on hand already. Your price may be higher than that of a competitor. These are among the many objections that will make an inexperienced teleseller, hearing them while talking with a prospect, conclude there is no sale to be made. Always in search of the "perfect" prospect, the novice will hang up and get on with the next call.

Yet in fact each of these objections, and most others like them, call for some further analysis. Consider these questions in response to the above situations:

1. Your prospect just bought the product (yours or a competitor's): "Are you happy with it? Does it do everything you expected? Do others in your household [or company] have a similar need for one? When will you be replacing it?"
2. The large inventory situation: "How fast do you consume your inventory? Can I help you dispose of that inventory [find another suitable user or, in a very aggressive move, buy it to make room for your product]? Do you have room to carry two lines? It will enable you to see which one sells better for you."
3. The price complaint: "Are you getting everything you want or need for that price? Would a product that does more for you be worth a little more to you?"

As you can see, every objection has a response. It may not overcome the objection, but that is not the point. You always want to test each objection with a response, to determine if it is real or merely a smoke screen to evade you and the purchase. If after you have given it your best effort you cannot overcome it, then go on to the next call.

How to Handle Objections

Effectively answering objections requires being prepared in advance. Your Objection Handbook will help you keep on top. Knowing that you are prepared to handle objections as they arise helps you to stay relaxed, confident, and unintimidated by them. You are free to be creative as you deal with each situation and deliver convincing answers.

While real objections are the ultimate challenge, and are the primary concern here, the techniques presented are appropriate for handling all objections. Regardless of whether they are stalls, misunderstandings, false, or real, the same general procedures apply: They require only that you adapt them to the type of objection you are confronting.

When you hear an objection, your first step should be to restate it. "Do I understand you correctly—you are hesitant to act today because you fear that in the event of an accident, you will have difficulty getting your claim settled?" is an objection restated in the form of a question. This tactic accomplishes several things: It shows the prospect you are not afraid of the objection; you are going to confront it head-on. Also, you are recapturing the initiative in the call, which momentarily passed to the prospect when he or she raised the objection. You also want to be sure you fully understand the objection. If you don't, your prospect will no doubt stop you again and explain it further. On hearing the objection restated, the prospect too is put at ease. Some of the objection's sting is gone. Finally, you demonstrate the desirability of a meeting of the minds as the two of you work out an answer together.

After you have restated the objection, secure agreement that you are both talking about the same thing before you proceed. Keep it brief: "Is that correct?" or "Do I understand you correctly?"

As the third step, you qualify the objection. Make sure it is a real obstacle to the sale, not just an excuse to put you off. Determine how important it is. Will you have to overcome it, or can you handle it by minimizing it? As during your earlier analysis, you should use questions. The answers you get will allow you to resume the guidance and direction of the call. It is important to the dynamics of selling that you stay on the offensive, not be put on the defensive. Use questions to learn the real reason for the objection. This is especially important in dealing with stalls and false objections, where the motive isn't apparent or reasonable. Ask, "Why do you feel that way about it?" or "How important is that to you?"

Questions will make the prospect stop and think. And the dialogue that ensues will give you valuable insights into their thinking at this point in the interview.

When you fully understand the objection, you are in a better position to answer it. Look upon this phase of the interview as a sincere effort on the part of both parties to reach an understanding. If your prospect wants and needs your product, and it fills that need, answering objections removes obstacles to closing the sale.

Once you have determined that an objection is real, you are ready to answer it. You do that with a mini action-getting presentation. Go back and reemphasize a benefit, or introduce new benefits that again meet the needs of the prospect. Never argue with the prospect. Instead, employ your most powerful vocabulary and be positive. Use words that inspire trust, that are believable. Resist the temptation to exaggerate or get carried away in your desire to make the sale. Remember, the prospect is constantly evaluating the quality of your information.

And stick to the basics. Continue to concentrate on the need and desire to buy, and spark further interest. You might say, "You are right to be concerned about claim service, Mrs. Wolcott. I am pleased to say our claim service is fast, efficient, and easy to call on if needed. We are available twenty-four hours a day, from anywhere in the United States."

Some objections, however, simply cannot be overcome. Perhaps the prospect has a long buying relationship with your competitor, one that has been very satisfying. In such an instance, you will have to employ what is called the balance-sheet technique to handle the objection. Borrowing from the accounting profession, you play up the pluses of your product and play down its minuses. You could, for example, say, "In the long run, don't our benefit A and benefit B present an attractive alternative to the product you are now using, making us the desirable choice at this time?" Avoid criticizing your competitor, but do concentrate on minimizing the importance of their benefits. The enthusiasm you have for your own company and product plays a strong role. You have to believe that what you offer is better than what the prospect already has. You may want to write out a balance-sheet reply to each objection listed in your Objection Handbook.

Finally, after answering an objection or minimizing it, close on it. Do this by asking for the prospect's agreement with what you have said. This should be done for each objection individually. If you have presented a sincere, straightforward, and reasonable answer, agreement should not be hard to get. Each agreement you secure brings you that much closer to the sale.

Remember, in every case, you want to follow the clean, professional process of restating, qualifying, addressing, and securing agreement on each objection the prospect puts in your path.

To apply this process to a scripted situation, you must first think about the sales calls you handle. What objections do you most frequently encounter, or do you anticipate encountering? Now use the preemptive technique, planning to address the objections as a part of your script. Build the answers into your script. Take up the process at the third step, and answer them as you would any objection: Stress the benefit to the prospect of accepting your point of view. Follow those statements by seeking acceptance. You will know you have got it right if you repeatedly hear agreement.

If your preemptive strategy is not working, and prospects are saying no most frequently, go back to the analysis you did in preparing your script. How can you reword it to more properly address the objection? Do you understand the source of the objection? Are you addressing it head-on? The benefit of a teleselling campaign is that you do get immediate feedback, and can quickly change your strategy or script in response to that feedback. Fine tune your script until the majority of calls go your way.

Finally, a word is in order about the role of your marketing strategy in countering objections. If you find that objections you cannot overcome continue to block sales, change strategies. If you have sufficient authority, you may want to seek out and offer a *premium* to the prospect for buying. The pre-

mium should be of a related nature, such as a free first issue to periodical subscribers, or a month's supply of a favorite home product to those using your
house-cleaning service, or a coupon good for $50 worth of gasoline to those
leasing their car from you. Another tactic can be the *discount pricing* strategy:
"Act now and you save 25 percent off the full price of the product." The discount should be substantial enough to make buying attractive—at least 10
percent. Finally, either separately or in conjunction with your premium or
discount, you may want to establish a *deadline* to the offer: "This is sent to
you for a free 30-day examination before you pay the invoice or you can return the product"; or "This offer is good only until the end of the month."
Again, the length of the deadline should be reasonable for the situation. Setting short deadlines to capitalize on people's absentmindedness or busy
schedules will be spotted immediately by today's sophisticated prospect.

If you are working for a company, of course, you may not have the authority to establish such marketing strategies. In that case, go to your management, fully explain why such a policy needs to be established, and seek
approval for implementing special offers to induce prospects to set their objections aside.

A Word About the Price Objection

One of the most frequently encountered objections is to price: "Your price
is too high," or "I can't afford it right now," or "Your competition is cheaper."
This is heard frequently by tellsellers in all businesses, whether dealing with
consumers or professional buyers, and you will have to learn to address it.

It should come as no surprise that you employ the same technique for
dealing with the price objection as well. Begin by restating the objection. It is
especially important to ensure that it isn't based on a misunderstanding, either
of the savings to be realized by the prospect if they will use your product or
of your pricing structure. A misunderstanding could lead them to incorrectly
conclude that they will be paying a higher price than your pricing strategy calls
for. Many price objections are based on a misunderstanding.

If it is a real objection, however, you want to assume the attitude that price
is in fact a reflection of the value received. The larger the gap between the price
you are asking and the value perceived by the prospect, the more often the
price objection will arise. If your product is in fact overpriced, you will have
a hard time overcoming price resistance, but you should begin by building the
perception of value received from the start of your call.

But what if your price is fair? In that case, let your prospect know that
you, your company, and the fine products and services you provide are all part
of that price. If it accurately reflects the product's value, you should once again
be selling benefits. And what benefits (or value) are you selling?

The product itself. All of the tangible and intangible benefits that you
have found in your product research.

What the product does for the prospect. In selling terms, the satisfaction
of whatever buying motives the prospect may have.

Your company. It stands behind the product. You may even want to integrate some information on your company, its strength and history of success, if this will be a factor in your sale.

The service you offer to customers with the product. This can be anything from a money-back guarantee to a full service staff that ensures customer satisfaction.

You. Buying from you, as a part of the process, can only be accomplished by buying from the company you represent. You are an important part of the sale, for all of the reasons covered earlier and later in this book. Your importance cannot be minimized, ever. But it is especially important to answering the price objection.

SELF INVENTORY	Yes	No
1. I accept objections as a fact of life in selling.	⎯⎯	⎯⎯
2. I restate the prospect's objections to ensure I understand them.	⎯⎯	⎯⎯
3. I keep a list handy of objections I've encountered previously, with the answers to them noted.	⎯⎯	⎯⎯
4. I answer objections with product benefits appropriate to the user.	⎯⎯	⎯⎯
5. After I have answered an objection, I secure agreement by asking a closing question.	⎯⎯	⎯⎯

For Thought and Action

How do you measure up on the performance goals of this chapter, as tested above?

Now that you've completed Chapter 9, how are you going to change your techniques?

Before going on to Chapter 10, have you begun your Objection Handbook, using objections you now hear or expect to hear?

CHAPTER 10

Asking for the Order

The Key

The goal of your entire call is to get *action*, whether that action is securing an appointment, closing a sale, or committing the prospect to some intermediate action. Throughout each call you must be alert for signals that the prospect is ready to act, and be prepared to react to these signals with a trial close. If you have received no such signals by the time you have completed your presentation and answered the objections that arose, you must employ an appropriate technique to close the sale, one that makes the sale a natural conclusion to the call. Whatever technique you employ, it all comes down to asking the prospect to buy. This chapter gives you pointers on how to tell the right time to do so. It presents various techniques for asking for an order, including both trial and final closes, to enable you to select the ones best suited to your call goals and selling situations.

Closing the sale, or obtaining some similar commitment to action, has been your goal from the start. Now here you are, having worked through the various steps in your call strategy—you got the prospect's attention; you analyzed his or her needs; you made your presentation; you successfully handled all objections. The next step is to ask for the order.

The Closing Process

Many people, well-intentioned about their teleselling career, fail because they are afraid to ask for the order. And yet, if you have covered all the steps in your selling system correctly, asking for the order or closing the sale should come as the natural result of the conversation you have been having with the prospect. You have been building the entire sales interview to the point of asking for the order. And when the goal of closing a sale guides your call strategy and conversation, and the prospect has stuck with you this far, he or she expects the next step to be a request to buy.

If asking for the order is such a natural step, why do so many people have difficulty taking it? The most common explanation is fear of rejection: being afraid that by finally asking the prospect to buy, the teleseller is confronting the ultimate NO of the call. "No, not today," the prospect may say. And where do you go from there?

In simplest terms, there are very few people who can successfully sustain themselves on a diet of constant rejection. Asking a person to buy takes a lot of courage when rejection is the overwhelmingly likely result. Being able to respond favorably in that situation, by asking why not and then proceeding to try again, takes both skill and determination. The conversationalist will stop when he hears "No!" The teleseller, trained in product knowledge, selling, and communication skills, tries to turn a no into a sale. Expecting and asking a prospect to buy is what marks you as a professional.

Some tellsellers lack confidence in the usefulness and value of their product. Or they may not feel the price is fair. Still others have not followed the buying/selling process, securing agreement to benefits statements and answering objections. When they get to the final step, they are at a disadvantage and perhaps feel their failure is certain. Any of these attitudes is, in turn, reflected in the closing techniques used. Finally, some haven't really come to see themselves as salespeople, having to close sales as a part of the responsibility of their jobs. For all of these reasons, some tellsellers freeze at asking for the order.

You are being paid to close sales. Your company needs those sales to continue in business. Review your importance to the company in Chapter 2 to reaffirm these two statements. In addition, your prospect needs the product you are offering, either for work or to improve the quality of his or her life. So a lot is riding on your ability to ask for the order.

You can do so at either of two times: when you pick up indicators, called "buying signals," that the prospect is willing to buy; or when you have completed your presentation and feel that you have answered any objections the prospect has raised.

Fortunately, many prospects tip you off when they are ready to make a buying decision. Throughout each call you should be on the lookout for their buying signals. Such signals can occur at any time during the call, but most frequently they surface either during your presentation (confirming that it is, indeed, action getting), or as you successfully answer any objections presented. If you are generating interest in your product, your prospect will give you signals. They should be taken to mean that it's time for you to ask for the order.

Buying signals can take many different forms, limited only by the products you represent and the type of prospect you are calling on. They are easily recognized, usually surfacing in the form of questions (or statements) that indicate the prospect is envisioning using your product. Buying signals are both specific and related directly to doing business with you. Be alert for such questions as:

- How soon could you make delivery?
- Can I use my credit card to pay for it?
- What would it cost if I didn't take the entire package, only features A and D?
- How much work is involved in getting it into operation?

• Do you guarantee I'll get my money back if I'm not satisfied?

Just as frequently, the buying signal can come in the form of such statements as:

• I'll bet I could even use it to do [some other function] as well.
• That sounds all right to me.
• I could probably cancel my existing contract the day after your product arrives.
• My neighbor said he'd had good results with it.
• I've needed something that does this for a long time.

What do your prospects say to indicate a willingness to buy? What buying signals can you listen for, or do you plan to listen for, as you handle your calls? Begin a list of them here:

1. _____
2. _____
3. _____
4. _____
5. _____

Learn to listen from a prospect's point of view (empathy again), interpreting their comments to recognize a willingness to buy. And when you detect it, go to a trial close as described below. It will either get you the business, or allow you to further qualify and answer their counterobjection. But always ask for an order when you hear a buying signal.

For example, suppose the prospect indicates interest by asking, "How soon could you make delivery?" Your thought-out-in-advance response may be, "Do you have your credit card handy? If you'll give me the number and expiration date now, I'll see that it's shipped today so you'll have it before the weekend. Will that be in time for your use?"

If the prospect says yes, go immediately to your wrap-up and hang-up routine (see page 92). If the prospect says no, you should seize the opportunity to ask why not. That question will stimulate objections. Using strategies developed in your Objection Handbook, secure future agreement by again bringing up appropriate benefits. Your trial close thus accomplishes one of two things: You may close the sale right there; or, the worst that can happen is that you will hear another objection, and thus have to secure agreement on that point of discussion and try to close again later.

Go back to the buying signals you wrote out earlier, select several of them, and for each signal write out a closing statement that turns it into a trial close.

1. _____
   _____

2. _____
_____
3. _____
_____
4. _____
_____
5. _____
_____

How to Ask for the Order

For the professional teleseller, asking for the order is not tricking the prospect into buying; it is a strategy for bringing the call to a close with a definitive and favorable buying decision. The alternative is a sales call where the prospect assumes the initiative and says, "I'll think about it and get back to you." You want the initiative and must not wait for the prospect to close either the sale or the call.

It is at this critical point in the interview, then, that you must ask the prospect to buy. But you don't, of course, merely blurt out, "Well, will you buy?" There are a number of more subtle, but very effective, techniques you can employ in a smooth, natural manner to get a buying commitment. Review them here to determine which ones will work best for you in the situations you face.

One highly recommended technique draws its inspiration from what your attitude should be throughout the call: the "assume the order" close. If the call flow indicates a meeting of the minds between you and the prospect, and agreement on selling points is frequent, you assume the prospect is going to buy. Some tellers carry this a little further and begin portraying, early in the call, situations wherein the prospect has already made the purchase. Such questions as, "Will you use this on all of your trucks, or only on those hauling toxic chemicals?" or, "Which of your present components will you replace first with our model?" can carry the cooperative prospect one step further toward the close by assuming the sale is made. Such a technique can be used in conjunction with those buying signals where the prospect is clearly envisioning the product in use. With a minimum of ceremony, and doing nothing to break the mood, you pick up on the signal and carry it through to a close.

Use caution in reading buying signals when using this technique. If you misread the signals and go to the assumptive close, indicating as much in your closing effort, you will come across to the uncommitted prospect as pushy. If, however inadvertently, you make the prospect feel pressured, the result will be the immediate raising of numerous other obstacles to the purchase. Objections will then be harder to overcome. Use your best listening skills, your empathy, and your sensitivity, when planning to use the assumptive close. If you do, and read the signals correctly, this can be one of your most powerful closing techniques.

A related technique is called the "ordering instructions" close. When your intuition says the time is right to close, tell the prospect how to follow your ordering procedures. It is as though you were handing your listener a contract to sign or a purchase order to approve. With confidence akin to that demonstrated in your assumptive close, you give instructions on how to initiate the order. It can be as easy as the insurance teleseller's saying, "Now, if you'll just do the following, your coverage will be in effect at midnight of the day we receive your check." If you are selling to a business, you may ask the prospect to get out the company's purchase requisition, and then help him or her fill it in correctly with an order for your product, including specifications, model numbers, catalog numbers, and so on.

Both of the aforementioned techniques are low key, grow out of the course of the call, and assume the prospect is showing signs of making a buying decision. It is, however, often necessary to help the prospect come to the point of making a buying decision. But high-pressure selling usually won't work with today's sophisticated consumer, and it is especially easy to get rid of a pushy teleseller: The prospect just hangs up. Yet pressure-free teleselling is not appropriate either. The middle ground to take is to adopt the attitude that you are helping the prospect make the best buying decision to meet his or her needs. If your product is, in your opinion, the most suitable one, your firm insistence on the prospect's need to go with that product will often be welcome. When confronted with a prospect who should buy but cannot make a decision, you must take the initiative and urge, encourage, even compel the prospect to act.

For many years the "choice close," forcing a "yes" answer by setting up two choices, both of which could only be answered with a commitment to buy, was recommended as a means of helping force a decision. Today, however, prospects—especially professional buyers—may be conditioned to resist this close, which has been overused. That is not to say it is never appropriate, especially as a trial close. But be sure the choices are not contrived just to get the prospect to pick one. If it is natural to present two or more options, and such an offer flows from the conversation, use it. An example would be to ask the credit-card customer if four monthly installments or one payment is preferred. When the prospect says he or she would prefer one payment, go on to write the order up.

Another technique that is especially useful in teleselling is the "offer close." As mentioned earlier, such a close can be an integral part of your marketing strategy, and is often called the "soft" offer. You tell the interested prospect, or remind the reluctant one, that there is no risk in trying the product. Hence, a magazine subscription can be offered "free" by telling the prospect, "I'll send you the next month's issue along with the invoice. If you are not satisfied, merely write 'cancel' on the invoice and return it to me." In a related move, appropriate to virtually any item for sale, you can set up a thirty-day money-back guarantee. If the prospect isn't completely satisfied, the item may be returned for a full refund. Or you can offer the option of not having to pay for the product for the first thirty days of ownership.

You can also close a sale by asking questions to nail down the details of the sale. This technique begins with modified choice questions, such as, "Should we write this up for you with the minimum-purchase-guarantee provision? The amount we have been discussing would qualify you for that special rate." Or, "What limits of liability coverage do you want on your cars?" When the prospect makes a positive choice, you have the buying signal you need to go on to close the sale.

Still other techniques exist. In the "summation close," for example, you summarize the needs you've uncovered, and show how the benefits of your product meet those needs. With such a strategy, you would proceed by saying, "We have seen that you need the following . . . My product does that for you by . . . The cost to you will be . . . Now let me tell you how to initiate the order." This close is especially powerful in those situations where throughout the call you have sensed the prospect's desire for your product. By summarizing the entire situation, you also help lay to rest that phenomenon known as buyer's remorse, the natural feeling a prospect has, immediately after making a buying decision, that he or she has made a mistake.

Earlier, in the section on handling objections, you were presented with the concept of the balance sheet. It works as a closing technique as well, especially in those instances where you are helping prospects to make up their mind. Walk the prospect through the benefits of the product being offered. Then ask whether it isn't true that the factors favoring your product outweigh those provided by the product currently in use, or by that of your competitors. Again, ask for the order when you hear a favorable response.

Select the techniques best suited to your selling situation and prospects. Outline one or more closing statements using the techniques you've selected. Repeat them aloud to hear how they sound, or say them into a tape recorder for playback and evaluation. As with other aspects of your call strategy, you want to have your closing statements thought out in advance, planned to be as powerful as possible, and available for immediate use as the need arises.

Learning closing techniques that work is an ongoing process. Talk with your colleagues about what works for them. Read the books on selling listed in the bibliography. Look to other sales books as well to pick up tips that apply to your work. Plan to use at least one closing technique in each call you handle, and practice that technique. Most importantly, condition yourself to ask for the order. And don't take the first no for an answer; carry on, gently but persistently.

"How do I do that?" you ask. "What happens when I ask for the order and don't get it?" Your natural curiosity should compel you to ask the prospect why he or she hesitates to place the order at that time. And as the prospect tells you, you may now actually get to the real or final obstacle in your path, to learn what else you have to do to get the business.

Once you have identified this objection, answer it as you would any objection—with one exception. This time ask, "Assuming I can take care of that concern for you, is there anything else keeping you from buying now?" If there is, you'll hear it at this point. Once you have uncovered the real reason for resistance and dealt with it, you are home with a sale.

Test this approach, and again gently resist taking no for an answer. You will find your sales increasing.

What if you finally don't get the sale? Before hanging up, draw on that sales axiom that says you should always exit with an opportunity to reenter. If you are working in other than the one-call close situation, develop a strategy to set up the opportunity to call back at a later time. This can take the form of a soft offer: "Mr. Brandt, I appreciate your time in talking with me about your situation. I am going to take the liberty of adding you to my mailing list to ensure that you are kept informed of new product developments here. When we offer a product more suitable to your needs, I will get back in touch with you." Or you can choose a more forceful course of action by stating, "I am going to send you some additional literature and a letter with some further thoughts for you to keep in mind. I will call you in two weeks to be sure you got the information, and see what your feelings are then."

Often the situation itself will dictate the wording of your reentry route. The prospect may have spelled out a budget cycle beyond his control, or hinted at some internal changes that make it natural for you to suggest a call back. If you are dealing with consumers, you may merely say you will keep in touch, and make a note to give that prospect a call back after a set period of time— say three months. Put these names in a prospect file if you think they are viable possibilities for such follow-up, and get back to them when promised. Finally, your situation may change, with added new products, restructured prices, or something else to make your offer more attractive for converting those marginal prospects into customers.

On the brighter side, if the call went exceptionally well, and you close the sale, use the opportunity to ask for referrals. Say, "Oh, by the way, whom can you recommend who might be interested in my products? I get a lot of business from referrals." Assure the prospect or new customer that you will keep the referral confidential if they so desire.

And congratulations are in order. Following your carefully thought-out call strategy, you have gotten that all-important order. You have made the sale. But don't talk yourself out of it. Immediately, your goal becomes to wrap up the call and hang up.

After closing a sale, you experience a sense of both relief and exhilaration. Relief comes from the natural nervousness you felt and in response to your continuing professional desire to do well at your job. Exhilaration should come from realizing you have been successful and are one step closer to (or even beyond) your goal. You may be tempted to chat a while longer with someone you've gotten along with so well. *Don't do it!* You are giving your customer time to change their mind. Even more damaging, you may say something off the cuff that causes them to rethink their decision. You want to speedily yet politely conclude the interview and get on to your next sale. You should have a thought-out concluding statement that shows your appreciation for their business. Don't forget to say thank you. Perhaps go on to point out that you are confident that this is the beginning of a long and mutually beneficial relationship. You must quickly and successfully disengage yourself in a courteous manner. Use the exhilaration you feel after a sale to close the next one.

As soon as you have completed a call, you should wrap up the handling of the paperwork and follow-up procedures. If you made a sale, you want to get the papers off your desk and into the right hands for processing. This will ensure that the new customer has a smooth and flawless experience with your company. As a further result, there is a good chance he or she will not only stay a customer, but will also refer friends, relatives, neighbors, or colleagues to your company, and perhaps to you.

List below the procedures you must follow to completely and successfully wrap up a sale:

1. _____
_____
2. _____
_____
3. _____
_____
4. _____
_____
5. _____
_____

One key to wrapping up a call is to maintain good organization. An organized wrap up will take a minimum of your time now, and save you time in the future. And completing the details of the sale you just made will let you concentrate better on the next call you handle. Does your list include completing paperwork? How about clearing your desk of material backed up (files, forms, product sheets) from the previous call? Don't carry work from one call over into the handling of the next.

You may want to put the checklist you've just developed on a card and keep it handy for review. Use it to check your work, to be sure you are completely finished with one call and ready to go on to the next.

SELF INVENTORY	Yes	No
1. I keep in mind, from the opening hello, that I will have to ask for the order.	___	___
2. I recognize asking for the order as a natural conclusion to the interview.	___	___
3. I am alert for "ready to buy" signals from the prospect.	___	___
4. I use a buying signal as an opportunity to try to close the sale.	___	___
5. I ask the prospect for the order as often as is necessary to get the business.	___	___

For Thought and Action

How do you measure up on the performance goals of this chapter, as tested above?

Now that you've completed Chapter 10, how are you going to change your closing techniques?

Before going on to Chapter 11, have you identified and practiced the closing techniques that will work in your selling situation?

CHAPTER 11

Building Obstacle-Free Communication Channels

The Key

> Good communication skills are a mark of anyone who sells for a living. Restricting your selling exclusively to the telephone poses some unique communication challenges and opportunities, for your entire productivity rests so heavily on your ability to communicate. You must give your attention to the common obstacles to communication, whether they are physical, verbal, or mental; isolate them, and learn to control and overcome them. This chapter discusses some of the most frequent obstacles to good communication, and presents steps you can take to overcome them. Your goal is to remove those so you can communicate your selling message as effectively as possible, achieving the results you want in an effortless manner.

To be a successful teleseller, not only must you know your product and use that knowledge, you must be skilled in effective communication. The major obstacles to communication that you will encounter may be grouped into three categories: physical, mental, and verbal. Each requires your attention, and all three can affect the mechanics of your work.

The Physical Obstacles

You may think you are ready to handle your calls, with everything you need at hand. But are there distractions around you that you can control, such as paperwork left over from the last call, or crumbs and half a cup of coffee from your break? Do other people wander by and ask you questions? If any such problems exist in your work area, you are not physically ready to handle calls. You can virtually be certain that something will go wrong and your planned, knowledgeable teleselling interview will go awry.

You want to keep "down time" to a minimum, and that requires that you eliminate the physical obstacles you may have erected or that may have grown up around you. Your job, during your call sessions, is to stay on the telephone with prospects as close to 100 percent of the time as is humanly possible.

Preparation is the most important key to eliminating these physical obstacles. Use the following as a checklist of steps you should take to free yourself of them.

1. Know what materials you need at hand; forms, product sheets, presentation outlines. See pages 30–31 to refresh your memory on what you need. Get this material together now and keep it together.
2. Discipline yourself to complete the necessary work that one call generates before you go on to the next call.
3. Keep your paperwork load realistic. Don't set up unnecessarily elaborate record-keeping systems. What do you absolutely have to record in order to meet your goals? Your job is to stay on the telephone, not to be the best form-completer in the world.
4. Take your break and lunch away from your work station if at all possible. If not, be sure all traces of each are cleared away before proceeding to your next call session. Coffee-saturated forms and sales tools are hard to read.
5. As you gain experience with what you are selling and how the typical call unfolds, lay out your materials in the order in which you use them. Don't leaf through papers as you talk with a prospect.
6. Do everything within your power to keep distractions to a minimum. Hang a real or imagined "Do Not Disturb" sign over your work area. It's not easy in a busy office, but you have to make the effort in order to get your work done.

The Verbal Obstacles

Next consider your verbal ability. The mechanics of speaking are just as important as the words you use (Chapter 13) and the voice that delivers them (Chapter 14). Do you talk too fast or too slow? Do you mumble? Are you understood by prospects, or are you frequently asked to repeat what you just said? Do you use clear, easily understood words and phrases, or do your sentences run on, peppered with multisyllabic technical words? Speaking mannerisms can pose serious problems for you as you try to communicate with your prospects.

One of the most distracting speech mannerisms is the unconscious use of such non-word sounds as "uh," "umm," "ah," or "er." These sounds originate from a desire to fill the silence that results when you are thinking about what to say next. To fill silences that you have been conditioned to regard as uncomfortable, you revert to some basic sounds. The result is noises that interrupt the prospect's thoughts.

Overcoming verbal obstacles takes concentration and continuous effort. Here are some tips on how to work on them.

1. Don't rush your delivery. Take your time. Integrated pauses can make you more understandable, and add emphasis to what you say.

2. Use your notes and sales tools to keep you on track and your prospect properly informed.
3. Check your vocabulary, grammar, and sentence length from time to time. Better, invite a friend to evaluate you. Are you easily understood?
4. Know what you are going to say, either from your experience with your presentations or from rehearsal. Try to develop the skill broadcasters have, of thinking five words ahead of their mouth.
5. When you must truly extemporize, concentrate on not making any sounds as you think. A prospect's interruption is not as distracting as your non-word utterings, and it may be to place an order.
6. Pace yourself to your prospect's rate of speech, talking no faster or slower. Either speed variation is apt to alienate the prospect.
7. Avoid small talk that takes you off the subject, necessitating a renewed effort to get attention and proceed with your sales presentation. While small talk may be helpful to establishing rapport, its place is at the beginning of the call, and then only if time allows.
8. Through your speech and mannerisms, convey the impression that you are a warm and friendly person to deal with. Demonstrating that you are not going to be a high-pressure caller but a professional teleseller will minimize the obstacles that remain as you work on them.

There are some things you may say or do that create obstacles to the rapport you have been trying to establish with your prospect, or erode it once established. Many of them may be serious enough to kill a sale, or silently alienate the prospect. What things do you know of, from your sales or personal experience, that can act as obstacles to both effective communication and rapport? Begin your list here:

1. _____
2. _____
3. _____
4. _____
5. _____

The list could become quite lengthy. Did you remember to include the mention of controversial subjects? If you bring them up you risk offending prospects. And if they don't like you, that dislike will extend to your products and company. Religious beliefs, sex, political preferences, even social behavior can be considered controversial topics. If a prospect brings up a controversial subject, comment in such a way as to avoid committing yourself to any position. You may work on your own time for a favorite political party, but your job as a teleseller is to sell products, not persuade voters.

Another behavior to avoid is the use of profanity in your conversation. Even such mild profanity as "damn" can offend some prospects. Don't risk the damaging result, not even with a prospect who uses profanity.

The same can be said for off-color or ethnically biased stories and jokes. While never appropriate in selling, they are especially dangerous in teleselling, where you cannot see prospects or their surroundings or work area. Mr.

Smith might not appreciate your ethnic slur on the Irish, even if his mother weren't named Murphy!

Your job is to sell product features, advantages, and benefits. That should be done in terms of such buying motives as convenience, cost savings, security, personal satisfaction. Benefits that satisfy needs are the subject a prospect wants to discuss with you. Leave the subjects that can create obstacles for you unmentioned.

The Mental Obstacles

All tellsellers face a number of challenges to their ability to go on with their work. Earlier it was pointed out that the telephone itself sets up some of these challenges. How can you "see" a call through to a conclusion when the prospect is only a voice on the telephone? How can you pace yourself to complete an entire call session when the work is repetitive?

Other mental obstacles to be overcome result from the nature of selling itself. These include dealing with nervousness, especially when trying to sell a stranger something over the telephone.

Do outside events influence your frame of mind as you begin work? You may be distracted by something not related to the call: a performance evaluation scheduled to come up at a time when you are behind your goal, or problems with a child or a disagreement with your spouse.

Personal prejudices can also hurt your work and results, whether based on sex, age, or national origin (race and religion are hard to determine by telephone). In a melting-pot nation such as the United States, you can ill afford to cater to such prejudices.

All of these obstacles can keep you from concentrating on what you are being paid to do: persuading a prospect to buy. You want to take the necessary steps to leave these distractions outside your teleselling work area.

One of the steps that can improve communication results from your attempts at being empathetic. Empathy will help you overcome distractions and prejudices. If you can envision the prospect as you talk with him or her you will be much more effective at selling. Try the following techniques:

1. Have an image (actual or imagined) of the prospect in front of you. This can be achieved in several ways:
   a. Go into the field, or attend conferences and conventions to meet your prospects and customers.
   b. Have a blank wall in front of you to allow you undistracted concentration on what the prospect looks like.
   c. Close your eyes while you talk with the prospect, or place a picture or two of your typical customer over your work area. By visualizing people as you talk with them, you can better empathize with their problems, needs, and concerns. And you will be better able to give them your full attention.
2. Remain calm as you talk. To best accomplish this, it pays to have your

work area well-organized. Remain in your seat and speak directly into the mouthpiece of your equipment. Control your voice. Your own calm will be contagious, putting the prospect at ease as well.

3. Develop your voice (see Chapter 14) to its maximum potential. You want to speak clearly, and vary the tone and pitch of your voice. Avoid a monotonous delivery, and put as much vitality and life as you can into each call you handle.

4. Be courteous. Listen, ask questions, don't interrupt. Take an interest in everything the prospect says.

5. Be genuinely sincere. It is not a coincidence that many major telemarketing operations set up headquarters in the midwest. People there are known for their warmth and friendliness, and the feeling comes over the telephone lines to put prospects at ease.

6. In your mind, put your prospect across the desk from you and talk directly to him or her, never breaking eye contact. This will enable you to talk in a natural, sincere tone of voice.

Pacing yourself through an entire call session, day in and day out, requires some planning. First, don't make the sessions too long. Two 3-hour sessions a day should be a maximum, if the hours spent are quality time on the telephone. Schedule breaks. Vary your activity, completing paperwork as you hang up after each call. Have a goal and meet it, whether it is calls per hour, presentations per session, or sales per day. Make *that* your objective, not the "three hours at a sitting." Reward yourself in some small way when you hit your goal. Keep interruptions to a minimum. Avoid the need to leave your work area for things you forgot. Have everything you need at your fingertips. Use these tips to help see you through a call session that is productive.

The Nervousness Factor

Do you get nervous at the thought of doing what you are being paid to do? Or while actually doing it? Then you might want to consider pitching ace Tug McGraw, one of the greatest relief pitchers in baseball history. Before the beginning of the 1980 World Series, he was asked if he was nervous about the prospect of facing the powerful hitters from the Kansas City Royals in the Series. "Of course I'm nervous," he responded, "I wouldn't be a professional if I weren't."

It is natural for you, too, to be nervous as you handle your calls. A lot is riding on you and how well you do. Remembering how important you are to your company, you know you have to make sales. And as a professional teleseller, you want and need to do well at your work. Your prospects, too, are counting on you to sell them the right product. If you aren't just a little nervous in the face of this responsibility, you should be.

Even your body responds to the pressure you are working under. Your pulse rate increases as your heart beats just a little faster. You may experience a shortness of breath. Nervousness is a natural bodily reaction to the pressure you feel when called on to sell something to someone, perhaps someone you've never talked with before.

Your attempt to deal with the surge of energy caused by your nervousness can result in behavior that may interfere with your selling effectiveness. Distracting motions, for example. Do you toy with a pencil or pen, or shuffle papers while you are on the telephone? Do you drum your fingers on the desk or elsewhere within hearing of the other party? Do you swing back and forth in your chair as you talk? These and other nervous motions may be perceived by the prospect and detract from your ability to communicate.

Obstructed speech can also result from your nervousness. You may fail to talk directly into the mouthpiece. Or you may talk too fast, slurring your words. You may talk in a monotone, or lower your voice to the point of being inaudible. These behaviors can betray your nervousness and seriously reduce your ability to communicate.

Another result of your nervousness can be those non-word sounds mentioned earlier. They originate when your brain is working and you momentarily don't have anything to say. Seeking to retain the initiative and not turn the conversation over to the prospect, you fill the resulting void with some sound, any sound, to keep from being interrupted.

Finally, you may find yourself resorting to the use of jargon or industry-specific terms in your sales calls. This is understandable. Using expressions common to your company or industry increases your comfort level. But your prospect probably doesn't understand your insider's language, and is more likely to misunderstand what you are trying to say. Avoid the use of jargon when talking with prospects.

Remember, if you do things to break the prospect's concentration or lose his or her attention, you weaken your chance to make a sale. So although nervousness is natural, you nonetheless have to concentrate on eliminating its symptoms when you are making a selling call. And the first step is to become aware of your nervousness-induced behavior. List the ways in which your behavior is affected or your nervousness exhibited:

1. Motions: _____

_____

2. Speech: _____

_____

3. Sounds: _____

_____

4. Jargon: _____

_____

You may again find it helpful to have a friend or colleague observe your behavior or even listen in on your calls, if possible. Or you can use a cassette recorder to tape your side of the interview.

Next, take steps to eliminate these behaviors, which over the years have become habits because you did not realize what obstacles they pose to your ability to communicate. Now that you are aware that they can cost you money, you should be ready to take steps to eliminate them.

Work on one behavior at a time to control the signs of your nervousness. For example:

1. Sit still. If necessary, get a stationary chair so that you aren't able to swing from side to side, or rock.
2. Keep your desk clear of all but the tools you need to do your job.
3. Have your sales tools organized in the order you will use them. Don't play with them.
4. Be conscious of your speech, and make the necessary adjustments to its volume and rate of delivery.
5. Have your sales interview planned. Rehearse what you will say, where appropriate. Keep the need for pauses to a minimum.
6. Discipline yourself not to use jargon, even in your talk with others in your company. It has no place.
7. Take a deep breath before you pick up the telephone. This will help you relax, and put needed power in your voice.

It will take a continuing effort to replace poor behavior with good behavior. Keep at the task.

Continue your self-evaluation and observation. Learn by watching and listening to others. Also remember that as your experience and self-confidence grow, your nervousness will diminish. Being well-prepared, having rehearsed your delivery, knowing your products and their benefits, and believing them to be valuable, you are not going to fail. You are the trained professional. Your prospect is going to listen to you, be friendly, and take an interest in what you say, even if you are not perfect every time.

Equally important to your frame of mind is your enthusiasm and your ability and willingness to let it show. Are you enthusiastic? Is it natural to you? And do you let it show? Are you confident about your ability to do your job, including selling skills, product knowledge, and ability to communicate? Or is there a nagging doubt in your mind about your skill in one or more of these areas? Are you prepared to do your work, with a plan you have confidence in? Do you believe you are going to be successful?

To address the shortcomings you may feel about your psychological approach to your job, you are going to have to first set priorities. What do you want to work on? Develop a plan and have the discipline to stick to it. Such a plan should consist of analyzing your work to identify your weaknesses, then reading, discussing, and observing others, all to learn what you must do to be more effective. It takes time to develop a proper frame of mind, and it takes experience to have the confidence you need for the long haul. Practice with the persistence needed to keep at it through the learning process.

What will eventually help you the most is getting on the telephone and talking to prospects. Your confidence will grow with experience. Believe in yourself, and in the good you do.

As one slogan would have it, "Don't worry; work!" The more calls you handle, the less time you will have to dwell on all those little doubts that can interfere with your ability to communicate and get the job done.

Up to this point, we have been discussing obstacles to communication on your part. But communication is a two-way street, and your prospect may exhibit some mannerisms that interfere with the process as well. When that happens, you, as the director of the course of the call, must exercise techniques to discipline the prospect, to keep the conversation on the path you planned as your call objective. Some of the problems you are likely to run into include:

- the prospect who turns out not to meet the company's guidelines, and thus is not eligible to buy your product
- the prospect who is very talkative, who seems to want to chat about any and every subject except your product
- the person who continually changes the subject, or jumps around asking about matters you would eventually cover if you were only allowed to stick to your planned sales call
- the person who mumbles, or talks too fast or too softly
- the person whose dialect or accent you have difficulty understanding

You can no doubt add to this list of "problem" prospects. Below list other people you encounter in your work who are poor communicators.

1. _____
2. _____
3. _____
4. _____
5. _____

Now consider your list and the one above it. What strategies and techniques can you employ with these prospects so they are not offended and thus lost, and yet are able to meet your call goals? Begin below to draw up a list of useful procedures to maintain control of the interview.

1. _____
2. _____
3. _____
4. _____
5. _____

You have a number of tools at your disposal to help guide and direct the call. First, keep your goal of closing sales uppermost in your mind. With a disqualified prospect, quickly but politely end the call. Don't waste time chatting with someone who cannot buy.

Your most valuable disciplining tools are questions. For the talkative, rambling person, resort to closed questions. You'll recall these require a one-word answer, and can often be used for the entire interview, enabling you to guide the call to a close in a minimum of time. Open questions, on the other hand, can be used when a prospect is not giving you enough information. With them, you can gently force lengthier, more descriptive, and useful answers.

If you encounter a person who gets ahead of your plan, you can try saying, "I'll be glad to answer any questions you have. But I intend to cover many of the things you are asking. Please bear with me." It is important for you to discipline yourself here, too, by sticking to your subject.

The strategy with a prospect who is difficult to understand is to repeat back what is said, to be sure you got it correctly. Don't proceed on assumptions. Jumping to conclusions can easily hurt you.

Disciplining your prospects to stick to your plan is an important skill for you to develop. It helps keep the obstacles to communication to a minimum, it allows you to get to your goal and on to the next call in an efficient manner, and it allows you to make the most of the short time you have with each prospect and use it for productive selling.

You can test a price or an offer, but there is no way you can measure the effect of communication on your sales results. You cannot attribute a lost sale to your nervousness, or your use of non-word sounds, or the way you have your work materials organized around the desk. You must just accept on faith that to be the best you can be, you have to be skilled as a communicator.

Remember, you are evaluated on the basis of your interest in your prospect, the quality of the information you deliver, your speech, politeness, and image. The prospect judges all of these things on the basis of how well you communicate by telephone. With that in mind, you must undertake to improve. Although you are not going to sell everyone you talk to, by working to stay on top of your skills, you improve the odds in your favor. Meet each prospect as a new opportunity to sell, respond to each individually, and have it in your mind that you are going to get the order.

SELF INVENTORY	Yes	No
1. I discipline my prospects to stay on the subject when the situation calls for it.	____	____
2. I have the materials I need on hand before I make my calls.	____	____
3. I don't interrupt the prospect, and I yield when he interrupts me.	____	____
4. The fact that I am nervous does not interfere with my call-handling effectiveness.	____	____
5. If I have to put a call on hold, I leave the line politely, telling the prospect how long I'll be.	____	____

For Thought and Action

How do you measure up on the performance goals of this chapter, as tested above?

Now that you've completed Chapter 11, how are you going to change your work techniques?

Before going on to Chapter 12, have you taken the steps necessary to remove as many obstructions to communication as you can?

CHAPTER 12

Your Positive Mental Attitude

The Key

All successful salespeople have learned to handle rejection as a fact of their professional life. In telephone selling, you will encounter a higher-than-normal rate of rejection by virtue of the sheer number of calls you handle. You have to develop confidence in yourself, your company, and your products in order to work in the face of this rejection. This chapter presents you with activities that demonstrate the power of your mind to exert an influence over everything you do, and suggests steps you can take to increase your positive mental attitude.

It is hard work to sit for hours contacting faceless people on the telephone, encountering rejection at a rate no other salesperson faces. Unless you are persistent and take steps to counter both the rejection and the monotony, you will become discouraged and set in motion a downward spiral of lost sales, greater discouragement, more lost sales, deeper depression, no sales, and finally despair. The key to avoiding this disastrous situation is your PMA: Positive Mental Attitude. It takes an effort to develop and keep one, but is worth it when you consider the alternative.

The Importance of a Positive Mental Attitude

There are any number of reasons why you want to keep your spirits up about your work, not the least of which is that you want to get satisfaction out of what you do for a living and enjoy yourself doing it. Your results, in turn, will be reflected by your state of mind.

One of the hidden factors at work in all human activity, and one with special significance to everyone in teleselling, is known as the Pygmalion effect. In Greek mythology, Pygmalion was a sculptor who was dissatisfied with every woman he had ever known. And so he created a statue of a woman so beautiful that he fell in love with her. When he prayed to Aphrodite that he might find such a perfect woman for his wife, Aphrodite did him one better: She brought the statue to life, thus enabling Pygmalion to marry his ideal woman.

The phenomenon of helping something come true by believing that it will is well-documented in other, more practical situations than Pygmalion's. A well-known study on education found that students believed by their teachers to have high I.Q.'s actually performed better at the end of one year on standardized tests, even though they actually were no brighter than their classmates. Similar studies among managers trained to believe in and expect the most of subordinates have shown the Pygmalion effect to work in business.

In sports, where mental attitude is an absolute requirement for excellence, examples abound. A pitcher with a lifetime winning record in the National League, claims not to see batters at all (a common assertion among pitchers). Instead, he envisions the pitch he is about to throw leaving his fingertips and traveling through a cone to the catcher's mitt. Jim Frey, a noted baseball coach and major league manager, urges players, many of whom have gone on to become the game's superstars, "Think, 'I am the best player on the field tonight,' and you will be. Lock that into your head, and nobody can take it away." As recently as April 10, 1984, an article in *The New York Times* entitled "Pygmalion in the Gym: Expectations Fulfilled," concluded that "expectations are widely recognized, at least among psychologists and educators, as a powerful tool to bring out the best in people." Sales managers and trainers share that finding.

Finally, consider the plight of the seventh duke of Medina Sidonia, in Spain. In the sixteenth century he wrote his king, "Sir, I have no health for the sea. I know from the small experience I have had afloat that I am always seasick and catch cold. I have no doubt that His Majesty in his magnanimity will do me the favor which I humbly beg, and will not succeed." The king lacking both magnanimity and a knowledge of the Pygmalion effect, failed to heed the request. The seventh duke went forward with his Spanish Armada to suffer the greatest defeat in naval history, at the hands of Sir Francis Drake and the British Fleet.

If you expect to fail at any activity you probably will, and anticipating success will help bring it. Envision yourself making a sale. Tell yourself you can do it, see it unfold before you in each call you handle, and imagine the prospect saying yes. In other words, if you think, "I am the best teleseller at work right now," you will be. If that thought is firmly locked in your head (and perhaps printed on a card placed over your telephone as a reminder), no prospect can take it away from you. You *will* close the sale.

Perhaps a demonstration will persuade you of the power of your subconscious mind to influence the outcome of events. That you can, as the practitioner of this activity put it, "put ideas into operation." Try the following:

1. On a blank piece of paper, using a disk about 4 inches in diameter as a guide, draw a circle. Then make a cross through it, with the lines intersecting at the center. It should look like the diagram on page 106.
2. Tie a light ring or key to one end of a string about four inches long. Hold the string between your thumb and index finger, with the key hanging like the weight of a pendulum over the intersection of the cross, about 4 inches above the paper.

3. Now think around the circle in a clockwise motion, following the circumference with your eyes and ignoring the key and string entirely. After a few moments, the pendulum will begin swinging around in the direction your eyes are traveling. At first it will swing in a small circle, but it will steadily widen out as you continue.

4. Next, *in your thoughts only*, reverse the direction to counterclockwise and follow the circle with your eyes in that direction. The pendulum will slowly change direction and eventually swing to a wide counterclockwise circle.

5. Now think up and down the vertical line. When the key begins to swing in that direction . . .

6. Shift your eyes to follow the horizontal line.

7. Finally, bring your eyes to rest on the point of intersection until the key has ceased its movement.

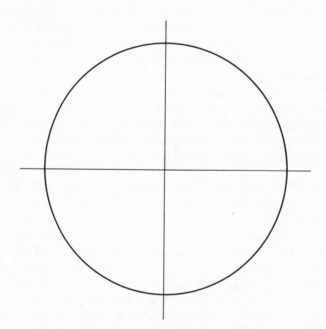

With each step, the pendulum will stop for a moment, and then begin to move in the direction of your thinking. If you haven't tried this experiment before, you may feel that there is something uncanny about the result. There isn't. It merely demonstrates how subtly your mind can influence your actions and therefore the outcome of events. There is truth to the axiom, "Wishing makes it so."

The relationship of a positive mental attitude to selling is obvious. Your attitude will affect your results. How you feel about yourself, your work, your company and its products, and, most important, your ability to do your work, all have an impact on how you come across to your prospect. Put forth a positive effort, have a positive self-image, and project a positive attitude toward your company and products. With this winning attitude, you will produce winning results. With the same persistence you employ to make a sale, resist negative thoughts and thus avoid negative results.

Do you know how your attitude affects your telephone contacts? Are you in a positive frame of mind for each call? Test yourself, both now and in the future, to reinforce positive behavior.

1. Is my attitude a positive belief that I am going to make the sale?
2. Is my attitude one of interest in the prospect?
3. Do I listen to the prospect?
4. Does my attitude reveal that I like the prospect?
5. Is my attitude that of a professional teleseller?
6. Is my attitude that of a successful teleseller?
7. Do I concentrate on what I am saying?
8. Do I communicate my ideas effectively?
9. Does my attitude reveal confidence in myself, my company, and its products?
10. Is my attitude optimistic and enthusiastic?

Your self-esteem is important to the frame of mind necessary for projecting a positive self-image. You should never feel guilty about calling anyone at any place or time to tell them about your products. You are performing a valuable service. If you lack confidence, answer the following questions:

1. Over the years, how much time have you devoted to learning all you can about your business specialty? (Include the time you will have spent completing this Self-Teaching Guide.)
2. How many hours have you spent acquiring product knowledge and/or learning specific product applications to prospect needs?
3. How many overtime and weekend hours have you spent servicing established customers and trying to educate new business prospects about the products you believe can be of benefit to them?
4. How many of your present customers and prospects actually care that you are dedicated to serving their needs to the best of your ability?
5. How many of your established customers have ever thought of apologizing to you when they call you after business hours to get your expert business advice?
6. What would be the consequences if prospects and customers failed to make use of your products?

The answers you wrote in response to these questions should convince you that you have helped (or will help) numerous customers who once may have complained that you were disturbing them. Now they are no doubt glad that you got in touch with them. Your satisfied-customer list should be a source of great satisfaction to you, and further persuade you of the value of your work.

Developing a Positive Mental Attitude

The first step in building a Positive Mental Attitude is to acknowledge the need for it and then accept responsibility for your attitude and results at all times in your work.

One of the qualities exhibited by successful tesellers is an entrepreneurial spirit. Regardless of the size of the organization they work for, they jealously guard the attitude that they are in business for themselves. As a broker for products, they face the universe on their own, to succeed or fail by their own devices. The products are perceived as unique, and because they are unique, there is reason to call every prospect imaginable to talk about them. With belief in the company and products represented, and in the value of selling those products to qualified prospects, they find it easy to get their selling message across. And they don't lose sight of the fact that they are the most important factor in the sale. They are the difference between making and losing the sale.

To insure your careful planning will produce results, you now want to stick to that plan, confident in the knowledge that if you do, you will be successful. As a professional writer commenting on his experience pointed out, "By merely setting goals, you have set in motion the force needed to see that they happen. When you set a goal and acknowledge it, you send the thought out into the universe. By so doing, you begin to make it come true." Require of yourself that you reach at least 10 to 20 prospects per hour. Set a success goal of giving from 5 to 10 full presentations in that hour, or of reaching at least that many decision-makers. Keep at it until you do.

Use a chart to track your results. Look at it every once in a while to convince yourself that you really are getting the job done. Over an extended period of time—a month, a quarter, a year—you will see that you have contacted 2,400 or 7,200 or even 28,800 prospects; made 600 or 1,800 or 7,200 presentations; and closed 200 or 600 or 2,400 sales in those periods respectively. When you get to feeling that a day just isn't working, look at your productivity charts and realize that if you will just keep picking up the telephone, you will succeed. The large numbers of prospects the telephone allows you to contact guarantees that.

You should be aware of your attitude toward the telephone itself. If you were trained at or are active in outside selling, you may perceive it as a threat to your livelihood. Don't. Nor should one who is new to selling, and using the telephone as his or her first sales channel, be intimidated by the instrument. It is only a tool for your work, like your paper, pen, or product kit. View it as outside salespeople view their automobile, as a device that carries you into the presence of the prospect, thus doing little more than extending your legs electronically. And it does that more efficiently and effectively than any other medium available to you.

One of the first things you have to sell is yourself: You must persuade the prospect that talking with you is worth the time. One of your objectives, then, to be worked on throughout your selling career, is to develop a personal public-relations campaign. List below factors that can help you sell yourself to your prospects.

1. _____
_____
2. _____
_____
3. _____
_____
4. _____
_____
5. _____
_____

Remember, too, that the company you represent and the products you sell will have an impact on your self-styled public-relations campaign. And your campaign will be strongly influenced by the fact you are selling by telephone, and thus not able to present yourself physically to the prospect. Your list should have included some of the following:

1. *Your image.* Earlier you were presented with image as a factor in your calls. This is created by things about you that lead a prospect to evaluate you even though you aren't visible.
2. *How you handle the calls.* Are you businesslike, behaving in a manner that reflects favorably on you and your company? If you hang up on annoying customers or argue with prospects, use profanity or engage in controversial conversation, you are hurting your chances of making sales.
3. *Your coming across as a friendly, helpful person, confident about your ability to be of service.*
4. *Voice and speech mannerisms that make a favorable impression.* Remember the admonition, "First impressions count." What impression are you making?
5. *Making only positive statements,* never negative ones such as, "I know you may not need this, but . . ." You also should never apologize for calling. You have a valuable product to offer. As an intelligent consumer, the prospect wants to be informed and thus allowed to make his own buying decision.
6. *Never calling the prospect by his or her first name.* This social error can be damaging. If you are having a drink with a prospect, calling him Bob would be okay. But as long as your sole contact is on the telephone, keep it businesslike and call him Mr. Jackson, unless invited otherwise.
7. *Being yourself.* You are part of the package that the prospect is buying. By being natural, you avoid appearing insincere and don't have to worry about maintaining some artificial role you assumed for the call.

These lists—yours and the one printed here—will serve you in keeping on track with a positive public-relations campaign, selling yourself to the prospect at all times.

Another point you should consider is how you ought to dress for your telemarketing activities. This subject is appropriate to the PMA chapter because the way you dress affects how you feel while on the telephone. Even though your prospects can't see you, your attire should be professional. As one man who worked with business prospects from his home in his pajamas put it, "I always felt as though I was outranked by the person on the telephone." Little wonder. If you are too at ease in your clothing, it may result in lax telephone behavior. Dressing appropriately can also increase your self-confidence.

How do you deal with long hours on the telephone, frequent rejection, and the sometime monotony of handling call after call after call? These problems plague all telesellers, but are especially acute among those who work from a script. The following suggestions may help you:

1. Take frequent breaks. To facilitate keeping to your productivity schedule, tie the breaks to your productivity goal, not the clock. After making sixty calls, or thirty presentations, get up and go to another area, have a snack, get some exercise, or otherwise interrupt the routine.

2. Vary your activity as it relates to your work. Again reacting to your productivity and not the clock, follow a call-handling period with an administrative period, doing filing, note writing, or planning for the next session. If possible, do this in a work area away from the one in which you handle the calls.

3. Figure out ways to inject variety into the work itself. Can you change scripts, or parts of scripts? Can you work a different prospect or customer base? Or undertake a different marketing activity, shifting from cold-call prospecting to customer service? Any change of work pace will help get through the three to four hours you put in on the telephone at any one time.

4. Ensure you have pleasant work surroundings. If you can design your own area, do so. At least decorate it with personal effects like pictures, mementos, plants. Some people recommend that you place in view pictures of the items that inspire you to work harder: the car you will buy with your commissions, or the gift you'll get a loved one when your bonus comes through. On this score, you may want to plan on a small purchase with some of the extra income you attain. In any event, your surroundings should motivate you to do your job to the best of your ability.

As with all professions, that of teleseller has a lifetime learning requirement. Begin immediately to develop the *habit* of reading helpful books. Go to your local bookstore or library and see what other sales professionals have to say. The bibliography at the end of this book includes a number of books devoted exclusively to teleselling. Your local librarian or bookseller can help you to find others. But don't limit yourself to teleselling books. All salespeople share many common problems and situations and require similar skills. Any books on selling will do, so long as you read them with an open mind.

You will reap several benefits from such a reading program. You will learn how other successful salespeople work. That can boost your confidence in your own abilities as a teleseller, especially when your behavior is reinforced by learning that other pros do the same things you do. In addition, you will pick up plenty of tips on what works. Whether it is items 3 and 7 from a list of ten successful closes, or an entire strategy for penetrating a new market, you can plug in what you read to what you encounter on the telephone. You are feeding your brain, and the ideas absorbed will be there to help you as you encounter new situations, different people, related activities.

And don't ignore books of a motivational nature: Napoleon Hill's *Think and Grow Rich*, Wayne Dyer's *Pull Your Own Strings*, and the highly regarded *Born to Win* by Muriel James and Dorothy Jongeward can all help you to boost your ego and your sense of self-control. Books can keep you on the track to continued success by equipping you with both the skills and attitudes needed to be a winner.

SELF INVENTORY	Yes	No
1. I am in a positive frame of mind and enthusiastic about myself, my company, and its products before I make each call.	——	——
2. Each of the calls I handle represents my best effort and highest professionalism.	——	——
3. I recognize that my attitude and actions affect how successful I will be in each call I handle.	——	——
4. I am friendly and helpful to and interested in every prospect, giving each individual special consideration.	——	——
5. I get back on the telephone quickly during my work sessions.	——	——

For Thought and Action

How do you measure up on the performance goals of this chapter, as tested above?

Now that you've completed Chapter 12, how are you going to change your techniques?

Before going on to Chapter 13, have you established a routine to acquire and keep a Positive Mental Attitude?

Using Words That Sell

The Key

The words used and how they are used are always important in selling. For you as a teleseller, they take on an especial importance. You are not able to rely on the force and influence of your physical presence, or your ability to demonstrate your product, to carry you to a close. Making use of the right words at the right time to qualify the prospect, present your product, and answer objections is critical to a successful call. This chapter will help you recognize good selling words and gain an understanding of the role such related factors as pronunciation play in the effective use of words in selling.

Throughout the sales interview, you are called on to use words well. You have the luxury of writing out, rehearsing, refining, and finally memorizing your attention-grabber. You can plan in advance how to phrase 90 percent of your needs-analysis questions. But when it comes time to deliver your action-getting presentation, and as you deal with objections, you must develop and employ effective language on the spot. Drawing from your memory, you plug words, phrases, and complete sentences in at the right moment. You want to condition yourself to make your language positive, descriptive, and confidence-building. Avoid negative, vague, or questionable words, as well as jargon and industry- or company-specific terminology.

Developing Word-Use Skills

The importance of your choice of words is the result of several factors unique to teleselling:

1. There is a time constraint. You probably have *at most* ten minutes with consumers and twenty minutes with business people to get your point across.
2. You are not visible to the prospect, and so cannot actively demonstrate your product or gauge your prospect's reaction to what you say.

You have to be sure, going into the call, that what you say will have the desired impact and provoke the needed reaction.

3. Your call is easy to interrupt or halt.
4. You don't know what may be going on around the prospect, or who else is there to distract your listener from what you are saying.
5. In most instances your prospect cannot handle your product, role-playing its actual use. You have to speak in terms that create an image in the prospect's mind of his or her actually using the product.

For these reasons, it is imperative that you give careful consideration to the language you will use in all of your talks with each prospect. Your language carries the whole message, playing a descriptive as well as a motivating role.

Before going into details about effective word use, a cautionary note is in order: Be yourself. Acquire and use only words that are natural to you and your selling situation. Be familiar with and thoroughly understand every word you use. Be sure you can pronounce them all correctly. In so doing you will go a long way toward inspiring the trust and confidence you seek of your prospects.

Naturalness, then, is one characteristic of the words that aid you in ensuring that your message is clear. Another is that the words used be simple and easy to understand. Be direct. Don't use "nevertheless" when "but" will do. You yourself will have to find examples of ways to simplify your vocabulary and speech habits in general. The key is, the more simple your choice of words, the easier you are to understand.

Precision in your choice of words is also important. Select words that enable you to say *exactly* what you mean, as concisely as possible. As you build your selling vocabulary, remember that your purpose is to communicate. Your prospect won't be impressed by or measure you on how complicated your vocabulary is. He or she will react, though, to how well the words you use get your point across. Your words should convey your ideas, no more and no less.

If you think you need to strengthen your vocabulary you should pay close attention to your daily conversation, both general and when you are selling. Try to catch yourself, and encourage others to catch you, when you use poor or inappropriate words or mispronounce words.

Keep a dictionary handy and use it. When you encounter a word you don't know, look it up. If it is a word you can use in selling, begin to use it only when you are sure you can do so correctly. Never use a new word for its own sake; use it only if it makes your communication more clear, concise, or precise.

While on the subject of word meaning and choice, a consideration of jargon is appropriate. Every industry, trade, and profession has developed language that an outsider could not readily understand. To see how harmful the use of such jargon can be to your presentation, begin compiling a list of terms you use in discussing your work with colleagues. These words or terms should have regular use and special meanings in your work.

Now, choose one person you know who is not connected in any way with your company or industry. Ask this person to define those words and phrases. Write down the exact definitions as they are given to you. Now compare the definitions with your own intended meaning. How different are they? Did the person even know what you were talking about? This activity should demonstrate to you how a partial or complete lack of understanding (which is worse?) can confuse the prospects you are dealing with. You must work to get jargon out of your language.

Distinguish, though, between jargon and legitimate industry phraseology, especially in business-to-business teleselling. The use of proper industry-accepted terminology enhances your professionalism and adds credibility to what you are saying. To avoid misunderstandings and the resulting dissatisfaction (or worse) on the part of the customer, you must use descriptive language that gets your exact meaning across. If technical language peculiar to your market helps do that, use it. But be sure it is language your prospects will have no trouble understanding.

You must also avoid such speech habits as slurring words, running words together, or dropping the endings off words. Slurring makes many words sound alike. If "burst," "thirst," and "first" are slurred, resulting in "burse," "thirs," or "firs," you will have lost the effect of a good word well chosen. Slurring will result not only in possible misunderstandings but in the prospect's forming a negative impression of you.

Do you run your words together in your haste to get everything into the time allowed? You'll find that if you say "Thebenefittoyouisthatyou'llsave severalthousanddollars," it is as hard to understand on hearing as it is to read.

Another example of poor enunciation is the dropping of endings off words. Saying "I'm gonna be writin' you a letter to confirm this and includin' some samples" gives the appearance of personal sloppiness. It can, by making you appear either lazy or uneducated, distract the prospect from your sales message to thoughts about what kind of person you are.

On the other hand, you may be mispronouncing frequently used words or adding unnecessary syllables, as when people pronounce "mischievous" as a four-syllable word, or say "irregardless" instead of "regardless." All of these and numerous other examples you hear daily (How often do you hear "nucular" for "nuclear"?) can lead to misunderstandings or even provoke irritation. Use the dictionary, and work on all aspects of your enunciation and pronunciation in order to be clearly understood.

Here is a list of words that are commonly mispronounced in selling: advantageous, government, comparable, miniature, mathematics, additive, economics, picture, advertisement, film. Be sure you are pronouncing these correctly. Choose a few words from your sales literature or presentation, and try this activity with them as well.

Another step you can take to improve your word usage is to read and write more. Newspapers, general and business and industry magazines, newsletters, and in-house publications will all introduce you to new words you can use to sell more effectively.

You can also use word books and handbooks of common usage to both expand your vocabulary and improve your sentence construction. Choose them from the bibliography at the end of this book, or go to a bookstore or library and browse. Look at *The Reader's Digest*, which frequently contains a feature entitled "It Pays to Increase Your Word Power"—an especially meaningful title for tellsellers.

Try writing out what you plan to say. Put on paper the key words, phrases, even sentences that you may plug into your otherwise extemporaneous action-getting presentation and answers to objections. Using a cassette recorder, tape what you have written and listen critically to the replay. Make the necessary changes and repeat the process until you have clear and concise wording for the key points you want to make. The writing process will force you to think carefully about what you say to each prospect.

To go back to a point made at the beginning of this chapter, words are vital to your success. Because you are working on the telephone, your voice and the words it speaks are nearly the entire basis of the prospect's evaluation of your contact with them. Remember, an effective speaking voice, as discussed in the next chapter, will do little good if the vocabulary isn't there to give it meaning.

The Words to Use

Your ability to express an idea is as important as having the idea in the first place. Words are the only sales aids you have in teleselling.

Attention here will be on the types of words you can use to sell more effectively. And as you might expect, the best words are those that convey benefits. Benefits, you'll recall, show how a prospect is going to gain from acquiring your product. The words "benefit" and "gain" are themselves examples of effective selling words. Other examples of beneficial words include "guaranteed," "ease," "economical," and "satisfactory." What words, perhaps used in your product literature, can you add to this list?

Words that show your sincere interest in the needs, problems, and concerns of the prospect should also be included in your vocabulary. For instance, "appreciate," "comfort," and "useful" will tell prospects you are thinking of them and not of yourself. Again, pause here and add words that you will use in your dealings with your prospects to the list.

You have read repeatedly here of the need to be positive about yourself and your work. Positive words inspire confidence. Describe your company's service as "efficient," your package as "complete," and your company as "reliable." Employ the principles of PMA in choosing how you describe your company and products, as well as in how you think about yourself and your work.

Telemarketing consultants Barry Z. Masser and William M. Leeds, in their *Power Selling by Telephone*, suggest you begin a "library" of words that invoke the image of action and thus get more sales. They assert that the words in the right-hand column below invoke a far more positive response than do the words to their left.

effect	*impact*
versatile	*multi-faceted, all-encompassing*
interesting	*colorful, fascinating, riveting*
quiet	*soundless*
economical	*cost-effective*
up-to-date	*state-of-the-art*
complex	*elaborate, highly detailed*
emergency	*crisis*
capacity	*potential*
skill	*expertise, genius*
hopeful	*enthusiastic*
trim	*sleek*
surprise	*astonish*
good	*fantastic*
better	*superior*
energy	*force*
difficult	*formidable, tough*
produce	*generate*
popular	*renowned, distinguished*
inflexible	*rigid*
dismal	*ominous*
unusual	*exotic, radical*

This sampling should get you started at improving the action-invoking power of your selling vocabulary. Review what you plan to say. Use a thesaurus to find words you could substitute for some you planned to use, words that would make your speech more lively (make that "sparkling"). A word of caution: Don't look for bigger words, ones you could misuse; just look for fresher or more vivid ones.

Always strive to be believable. Don't use superlatives. There can be only one "greatest," "finest," or "best," and these are relative to needs and benefits anyway. Besides, all these words are overused. Calling something the "newest" will only be accurate for a day or two in today's competitive market. Employing such a clichéd tactic can only erode the perception of accuracy you have been striving to establish. Believable words such as "dependable," "excellent," or "permanent," when backed by some statement of proof, convey a positive image without going to extremes.

Be sure to use words that reflect your enthusiastic attitude toward what you are selling. You are a "thorough" person, your product "complete," and your service "exceptional." Not only do such words convey your confidence and enthusiasm, they generate similar feelings in prospects. This will reassure them of the correctness of doing business with you.

Words that are descriptive of your product in use or that help the prospect envision the product are also important. Animated words, ones that dramatize the product and its benefits, will help you here.

In all instances, you want to select words that present your product in its best light. A final tip to help you is, where possible, to employ the same terms used by the prospect in describing his or her needs. If, during the analysis the prospect uses the term "trouble-free" to describe a desire for convenience, use that term in your presentation. You may have planned to pick up the phrase "low maintenance" or "maintenance-free" from your sales literature, but in this case "trouble-free" will have a greater impact.

And to ensure that all benefits are evident to the prospect, use clarifying or summarizing phrases like, "What this does for you is . . ." or, "For you, this means . . ." Again, wherever possible use phrases, words, or expressions the prospect has mentioned as important.

Finally, choose precise words to get your exact meaning across. For example, instead of saying yours is a "good" company, you could describe it as a "reliable, capable, stable company with a history of service to its customers."

This discussion has been proceeding on the assumption that you cannot demonstrate your product because you are selling over the telephone. But numerous tellsellers, both consumer and business-to-business, do in fact put on demonstrations over the telephone. Some, like textbook publishers and stationery and greeting-card manufacturers, send the actual product before the "ask for the order" call. Others, such as photographic studios and housewares manufacturers, may precede the call with a sample and illustrative materials. And many companies send catalogs. What can you put in your prospect's hands, prior to your closing call, that will help you dramatize as fully as possible how your product meets his or her needs?

But placing an object (or literature describing it) in the prospect's hands does not relieve you of your obligation to present the product thoroughly and forcefully. You now have to be prepared to sell in two completely different circumstances: If the prospect has your material or product in front of him, you will execute one call strategy. Or your prospect may allege, correctly or incorrectly, that material was never received. That forces you to resort to a very different call strategy.

A few last words about your speech: In addition to finding and using the correct words, you should be aware of your grammar and your sentence construction. Either poor grammar or bad sentence structure will detract from your selling message just as much as inappropriate word choice, use of profanity, or any of the other obstacles discussed in Chapter 11. If you are unsure of yourself in either of these areas, a good handbook of basic English will give you the needed guidance. You should keep one of these basic references at your fingertips. It will help you with correspondence as well as with spoken sales messages.

Be conscious of the words you use and the message they convey. Reviewing the types of words presented here, plan your sales messages to pack the maximum punch. After all, your words carry the entire burden of expressing your sales message and getting you to your goal of closing sales.

SELF INVENTORY	Yes	No
1. My vocabulary is appropriate to my task and my audience.	___	___
2. I help my prospect "see" what I am talking about with vivid, descriptive words.	___	___
3. I do not use slang, jargon, or unnecessary technical terms in my sales interviews.	___	___
4. I use words that convey a positive, empathetic, and sincere image.	___	___
5. I use the correct pronunciation for all the words in my selling vocabulary.	___	___

For Thought and Action

How do you measure up on the performance goals of this chapter, as tested above?

Now that you've completed Chapter 13, how are you going to change your word-use techniques?

Before going on to Chapter 14, have you developed your own list of action-inducing words to use in your teleselling?

CHAPTER 14

A Teleselling Voice

The Key

It is your voice over the telephone that carries your and your company's image to the prospect. To work for you, your voice must be clear and audible, its tone and volume well controlled. Working to develop a good selling voice is an important factor in a teleseller's obtaining results. This chapter shows you how to analyze your own voice to determine your strengths and weaknesses, and how to work on improving it.

$\mathbf{Y}$ou can see how important your voice is in teleselling when you consider that probably all communication between you and your prospect is spoken. Your livelihood virtually depends on your voice.

What Kind of Voice Do You Have?

What is your voice like? Are you easy to listen to? Do you use interestingly varied inflections? Does the tone of your voice modulate with the information you are delivering? Are you enthusiastic? You can learn the answers to these questions by completing a simple activity.

To proceed with this chapter you should have either a cassette recorder or a colleague to help you. You also need the outline of one of your action-getting presentations, one that takes approximately 3 to 5 minutes to get through. If you do not have one, either go back to Chapter 8 and prepare one, or find a section of any book that contains lengthy passages of dialogue. If you are already working on the telephone, you can set your cassette recorder by your telephone and record one of your sales interviews. What you want is a recording of your voice in a selling situation, or, if a friend is assisting you, sufficient material to give a 3- to 5-minute sales presentation.

If you are not taping your side of an actual sales interview (or, with the prospect's permission and the equipment required by law, an entire sales interview), take care to simulate, as closely as possible, the actual teleselling situation. It may help if you talk into a telephone handset (be sure to tape down one of the activator buttons to prevent the line-unattended tone, or unplug your phone if possible). If you are employing the services of a colleague, sit back to back and again use a handset. Don't look at each other. Actually, taping is the preferred method (though you can use both for even better results). The greatest value of this activity will no doubt come from hearing your own voice, perhaps for the first time, as a listener and from the prospect's point of view.

When you have your sales inteview prepared and the needed equipment and/or colleague present, tape your sample segment.

Now turn your attention to the checklists below. Either listen to your tape and complete both evaluation lists, or have your colleague do it for you.

EXTEMPORANEOUS-DELIVERY CHECKLIST

Indicate those characteristics your speech exhibits or lacks during this activity:

EXHIBITS	QUALITY	LACKS
_____	naturalness	_____
_____	enthusiasm	_____
_____	interest	_____
_____	good pacing	_____
_____	knowledgeability	_____
_____	spontaneousness	_____
_____	proper volume	_____

VOICE-INVENTORY CHECKLIST

Regard each line below as a sliding scale from one extreme to the other, and indicate with a check mark where on each you think your voice falls, judging by the test you made.

monotonous	varied
harsh	soothing
hostile	friendly
contrived	sincere
garbled	clear
dull	colorful
unpleasant	pleasant
halting	authoritative

You now have the material you need to go on to the next section. As you do, keep in mind that yours is the voice of your company. How do you sound?

To Develop a Selling Voice

How can you go about acquiring the vocal characteristics you need? This, like other roads to self-improvement, starts with self-awareness and self-analysis. Listening to your own voice is the start, but you must then work to improve it in ways that will make you more effective.

A voice characterized by many of the positive qualities listed in the last section is a prerequisite for effective teleselling. The self-analysis you just completed should have helped determine your strengths as well as your weaknesses. Once identified, these will guide you in starting your self-improvement program. Unless you have serious deficiencies in numerous areas, don't be put off. You don't have to be perfect, nor is it recommended that you retain an individual speech instructor (a public-speaking course *can* help) or begin with oral surgery. Instead, work on the basics. Your goal is not to become a professional announcer, but to be a more effective teleseller.

One of the problems everyone faces to some degree when talking on the telephone is a tendency to talk in a monotone. This results from the fact that you are not face-to-face with the prospect. A similar problem can arise if you are delivering from a script or have memorized your entire talk: You may be using a monotone or a singsong voice. Frequent repetition of routine data during your qualifying phase, answering often-raised objections, or after you have gotten the order, the need to fill out the necessary forms over the telephone can all sap the enthusiasm from your voice.

To overcome a monotonic delivery, play a simple mental trick on yourself: Envision the prospect sitting across the desk from you. Talk to the image and not to the telephone. Also, vary your routine so you don't do everything the same way on each call you handle. Call different types of prospects—first leads, then cold calls, then customers—if you can. And remain enthusiastic. Each call is an opportunity for you to demonstrate your personal excellence, and to make a sale.

Is your voice harsh, making you appear hostile or unfriendly? An antagonistic edge to your voice will put people off, and the resulting defensive attitude will be hard for you to penetrate. Similarly, if your sincerity sounds contrived, either because it is or because you push your friendliness beyond acceptable bounds, you will unnecessarily raise obstacles. A soothing, friendly, sincere voice will put prospects at ease, increasing their trust and confidence in you. To achieve that effect, begin by thinking a smile. If you smile while you are talking, you will give your voice a sincere, helpful tone that will encourage your listener to pay attention to what you are saying, as well as build that needed confidence.

Another potential problem for the untrained or undisciplined teleseller is rate of speech. How about you? Do you talk too fast or slow? If you talk too fast, you are apt to give the impression that you are the stereotypical salesperson, a "fast talker." That will have devastating consequences for your credibility. And yet, slowing down too much is likely to make your prospect impatient, and encourage cutting your call short.

You have two choices in determining how to pace your rate of speech: First, and preferred, is to match your rate of speech to that of the person you are selling to. That is, speak slowly and deliberately with those prospects who do likewise, and more swiftly with the fast-talking prospects. If you haven't mastered that skill yet, aim for the middle: Vary your rate of delivery. Be crisp and businesslike when analyzing needs, methodical and patient when reviewing details, and enthusiastic when describing benefits or while asking for the order. In every instance you want the rate of your delivery to work for you, not against you.

Is your speech garbled? Do you talk too quietly to be heard? Or so loud as to annoy? All three errors are common enough for you to be on guard against them. Do you chew gum while on the telephone? Or sneak a sip of coffee while the prospect is talking, then have to speak before you've swallowed it? These won't help your speech. You want to speak in a crisp, distinct, well-modulated voice. Employ a normal tone, speak directly into the mouthpiece, and be conscious of volume. Remember, the prospect is right across the desk from you.

Are you a colorful speaker? Do you create interest and draw attention when you speak? An expressive voice will help you get and keep the attention of your prospect. To be more expressive, raise and lower your voice, avoiding a monotone. Select key words and phrases to receive emphasis as needed. Vary your inflection and pitch to give variety to your conversation. Another ingredient in a colorful voice is vibrancy. An excited, vibrant voice that reflects your enthusiasm will help build interest in what you are saying. The more enthusiasm and excitement you have, the less "canned" you will sound.

The key to having a pleasant voice is to be natural. Don't try to force sudden or drastic changes, either on yourself or your voice. Learn instead to bring out the best in both. Being relaxed and natural is important if you are to project an image of sincerity. If you adopt forced speech or voice mannerisms, it will be apparent to the prospect and will damage your credibility. To project a pleasant voice, find your natural tone in the middle range of pitch possibilities. You can then manipulate the pitch up and down as the situation demands. Use the full range of the scale for maximum impact.

Finally, speak with the authority that comes from your Positive Mental Attitude and confidence. You are the professional in the conversation. You know your product better than the prospect, and your prospect needs the product, perhaps without knowing it. You are the one who is trained in the basics of selling, and you are doing a job very few people can do well. Let those facts show in your teleselling calls. You are the expert.

In spite of the large number of calls you handle, you must sound fresh and credible, as though each prospect is the first and most important person you are talking with that day. A well-developed voice will allow you to avoid giving the impression that you are mechanically running through a canned presentation. By delivering a natural-sounding and enthusiastic presentation, from your hello to your good-bye, you will close more sales. Once you can do this, you will appreciate the value of your voice as a tool.

SELF INVENTORY	Yes	No
1. I am comfortable while speaking with other people.	——	——
2. I conduct my sales interviews in a spontaneous and enthusiastic manner.	——	——
3. I speak clearly and what I say is understood.	——	——
4. My voice reflects a friendly, helpful, courteous, and understanding attitude.	——	——
5. The rate and volume of my speech are under my control.	——	——

For Thought and Action

How do you measure up on the performance goals of this chapter, as tested above?

Now that you've completed Chapter 14, how are you going to change your technique?

Before going on to Chapter 15, have you identified the characteristics of your voice that need improvement and developed a plan to work on those improvements?

Effective Listening

The Key

> Telephone communication, like all two-way conversations, requires listening to what is said. Effective listening ensures that you learn everything you need to know in order to sell your product. This chapter will help you determine whether or not you are really listening to your prospects. Then techniques are presented to improve your ability to listen. In this way you will uncover many opportunities to make better, more, or larger sales.

Many people, especially those who have never sold successfully for a living, have an image of salespeople as "good talkers." Or worse, as "fast talkers" in a pejorative sense, as if the term "con man" were derived from "conversation" rather than "confidence." Sales professionals, though, know better. It is the effective *listener* who succeeds most often. And as a teleseller relying almost exclusively on oral communication, you must master this *receiving* skill to complement your *sending* skills if you are to maximize your success.

Are You Listening?

To become an effective listener, you must keep the difference between hearing, and listening in mind. Hearing is a physical reaction to sound waves, wherein these waves are translated into understandable signals for the brain. You are hearing things at all times, both signals you want to receive and many you don't. Listening, on the other hand, is an active process in which you consciously pay attention to what you are hearing.

The following are some clues from your own behavior that indicate you are not as effective a listener as you should be.

1. You rely on heavy note taking, trying to get everything said written down. The goal becomes "get it down on paper," not "listen to what is being said."
2. You have little or no reaction to what the prospect is saying, but mechanically run through each call. The result: a lot of short calls.
3. You tend to tune the prospect out, race ahead mentally to what you will say later, or daydream about what you will do during your break.

4. You find yourself reacting only to preselected words or phrases that snap your attention back onto the call; then you wonder, "What did he just say?"

Other clues that you are not listening will be delivered by your prospects. They include:

1. Comments such as, "As I told you earlier . . ." or "I said . . ."
2. Frequent objections, which indicate you didn't hear the prospect's real needs and buying motives.
3. Fewer than average closed sales. You should, overall, close at least one qualified prospect in three.
4. Repeated questions from the prospect asking you to cover the same ground, indicating that you haven't heard what was really being asked.

If you detect any of these signals in your work, consider yourself properly warned that you aren't listening as carefully as you ought to be.

There are other behaviors on your part that become virtual "interview killers." The following checklist was developed by *Specialty Salesman,* and repeated in Mona Ling's classic, *How to Increase Sales and Put Yourself Across by Telephone.* Are you guilty of the following behaviors?

INTERVIEW KILLERS	Yes	No
1. Finishing the prospect's sentence for him.	___	___
2. Inserting your own "pet" word or phrase if the prospect hesitates.	___	___
3. Trying to rush a prospect who speaks slowly.	___	___
4. Showing impatience at any time.	___	___
5. "Educating" your prospect over the telephone, which may invite questions you can't answer at that time.	___	___
6. Talking while the prospect is talking.	___	___
7. Failing to respond to indicators of attention or interest.	___	___
8. Estimating inaccurately the degree of emotional involvement or suggestibility in the prospect.	___	___
9. Projecting your own fears, opinions, insecurities, or thinking on the prospect.	___	___
10. Correcting the prospect in mid-sentence.	___	___

If you put more than two checks in the yes column on this activity, or if you detected some recognizable signs in the poor-listening clues listed earlier, you'll want to give serious attention to improving your ability to listen.

Techniques for Improving Listening Skills

A lot of things interfere with your ability to listen effectively and truly hear what is being said. The obstacles identified below are some of the more common ones, easily dealt with by you without seeking outside help or making extensive changes in your work environment.

Inexperienced tellsellers seem to think it is necessary to talk to their prospects rather than listen to them. They may have been trained by someone who gave them bad advice, or they may be modeling their behavior after some of the poor salespeople they have encountered. Even when prospects assert themselves and try to say something, the teleseller may interrupt to express his or her own point of view. Then, when the sale is lost, the teleseller erroneously concludes that the prospect wasn't qualified. In fact, it was the prospect who was dealing with someone underqualified.

As you know from your own experience, when interrupted you become annoyed and, if it occurs more than once, frustrated. You want to end a conversation that is frequently interrupted as soon as possible. In a similar way, if the prospect has something to say, you can safely conclude it is important to him or her. By cutting in or cutting off, you not only miss a key opportunity, you alienate.

A teleseller who has developed listening skills knows not to interrupt a prospect. If you are presently in the habit of interrupting, it will take self-discipline to overcome the tendency. Once aware of your tendency to interrupt, concentrate on not doing it. Strive to lessen the number of times you do so. Pause after each call, review how you behaved, and renew your vow not to interrupt the prospect unless it is absolutely necessary.

Another frequently encountered obstacle to effective listening is lack of concentration, whether on your part or your prospect's. This can result from trying to do two things at once: Perhaps you are wrapping up the paperwork from a prior call while handling a new call, or having a snack while continuing to talk to prospects. What other activities do you engage in while you are talking on the telephone? There is an endless variety of things you could be doing that break your concentration on the call you are handling at the moment. If you compile a list of things you do that interfere with your concentration, you will increase your awareness of this problem. It is important to control your work environment as much as possible to ensure that it is free from distractions. Interruptions of all kinds should be kept to an absolute minimum. If you eliminate interruptions and distractions, you are free to concentrate on each call, one at a time, and on exactly what is being said.

Your attitude can also be an obstacle to effective listening. Do you get the feeling, "I've handled a thousand calls just like this?" Taking your work, prospects, or calls for granted, or behaving as though your activities will be routine, can lull you to sleep. And remember the Pygmalion effect. If you believe a call is routine, it will be. With such a mind set, you will stop listening.

Your best defense against this problem is to look upon each call as the unique opportunity it represents to make a sale. No two calls are alike. You know that. Be prepared to handle each call as a new, exciting, and separate activity.

Are you a prejudiced person? Do you hold people's race, religion, sex, or national origin against them? Of course not. So why do you react as a bigot might when your prospect turns out to be a customer or prospect of your major competitor? Or when they are in an industry, activity, or area of the country you have not succeeded with in the past? Product or market prejudice—jumping to conclusions about the likelihood of your success when you hear where your prospect is from, or what he or she is interested in, or who your competition is—can be a powerful barrier to listening. Instead of concentrating on what is being said, you tune out the prospect because you believe you are not going to get the order.

To overcome prejudice of any kind you must keep an open mind. It is no different in selling. Take prospects as they come to you and realize you offer a valuable product for them to consider. If you are going to draw any early conclusions, let them be that the prospect will buy. But most important, listen for opportunities to sell. Overcoming objections and getting qualified prospects to buy is hard enough; don't make it harder by deciding no for them before they do.

A final obstacle to listening could be your lack of interest in what you are doing or what you are selling. If your enthusiasm diminishes, or you are overly preoccupied with other things, or you haven't made a sale in the last fifty calls, your interest in your work, your product, or your prospects can wane. When that happens, you stop hearing what is being said and begin reacting to your prior experiences rather than to what is really going on. A loss of interest can make it difficult to effectively hear what is being said.

If you find this happening, pause a minute and take a deep breath. Take a brief break, and go to another area, away from your work station. Or undertake a different activity—do some paperwork or move from selling to prospecting. Pull yourself together. You will only be as successful as your attitude and enthusiasm allow. Keep them intact.

One of the benefits of improving your listening skills is that you will be able to hear more opportunities to sell. This can happen in several ways.

For example, you will hear which benefits to stress and when to stress them. How many benefits could you apply if you were an automotive-insurance teleseller and heard the prospect say, "Well, my current coverage expires in only three weeks"? Or if your cold call to an office manager, a prospect for your stationery company, produced the comment, "I always get my supplies from John Myer with ABC. He takes care of us every month"?

You will also hear many opportunities to create a need or desire. What would you say to create a need when you hear a prospect say, "I have enough of this stuff to last me the next six months. I'm overstocked already"?

Finally, you can learn, just from their conversation, what interests or concerns prospects most. Listening for what are referred to as "hot buttons," you will know which ones to push, to continue the metaphor, in your active presentation. For example, what would you stress to a person who comments over and over again that he is tired of doing business with companies that cannot service their customers satisfactorily? (That concern could be the real message he is conveying when he says, "Companies aren't run like they used to be.")

List below opportunities you hear from the comments your prospects make.

1. _____
_____
2. _____
_____
3. _____
_____
4. _____
_____
5. _____
_____

How can you handle each of the opportunities you listed? Spotting the needs represented in prospects' comments, then presenting benefits to meet those needs, is teleselling professionalism at its best. It demonstrates your interest in your prospects and their well-being, as well as your skill at providing service. With the examples presented above, remember the following:

1. The person whose policy is about to expire will respond well to the benefits of your immediate coverage put into effect with a minimum of inconvenience. The monthly service feature of your competitor can be turned to your advantage if you ask how they get something they need between visits and point out that you are as near as the telephone.
2. Stress to the person with too much inventory that your automatic shipments, tied to order history and adjusted on the basis of each subsequent order, will ensure they are never overstocked like that again. Ask if the money thus saved and space provided for more inventory of a different nature couldn't translate into more and better sales.
3. Obviously, the repeated complaint offers you a chance to stress your toll-free number or twenty-four-hour answering service, or similar provisions of your company's marketing strategy, without asking specifically about service. You have heard a need without prompting and then sold a benefit without even having to stress it.

One final plug, too, for the importance of a call strategy. Hearing and responding to these situations and to the ones you listed illustrates the need to have a call strategy committed to memory. Only when you automatically handle your strategy without conscious effort will your attention be free for listening for and hearing these all-important opportunities to sell benefits.

Listening is a two-way street. You can control your end of the communication bargain by concentrating on what you are doing, by keeping an open mind, by being mentally and physically prepared for each call, by demonstrating your interest in your work, product and prospect, and by not interrupting. These qualities inspire the prospect to be a better listener as well. If you are enthusiastic and empathetic and make the effort to serve your customers' needs, you will find your prospects pay attention to you. Your overall professionalism will then carry you to more closed sales.

SELF INVENTORY   Yes   No

1. I wait for the prospect to hang up first after we
have said good-bye.   ____   ____
2. My work area is free from distractions, allowing
me to concentrate on each call.   ____   ____
3. I pay attention to what each prospect is saying
throughout the call.   ____   ____
4. I listen for unexpected opportunities to sell a
benefit or create a need.   ____   ____
5. I am conscious of both what is said and what is
left unsaid, and consider their total to be the prospect's message.   ____   ____

For Thought and Action

How do you measure up on the performance goals of this chapter, as tested above?

Now that you've completed Chapter 15, how are you going to change your effort to listen?

Before going on to the performance evaluation test, have you identified those areas of effective listening in which you are deficient, and formed a plan to work on improving them?

Performance Evaluation Test

Among the traits and abilities you will need to succeed as a teleseller, those listed below are of prime importance. Using numeric values as indicated, rank each factor listed. Use the number that best reflects your assessment of your own work. After you have filled in all the blanks, add each column and record the totals for future comparisons.

IMPORTANCE	NUMERIC VALUE	LEVEL OF PERFORMANCE
None	5	Rarely
A little	4	Occasionally
Average	3	Average
Significant	2	Frequently
Vital	1	Every time

FACTOR	IMPORTANCE	LEVEL OF PERFORMANCE
1. **Mental comfort:** I am in a positive frame of mind. I believe I have a valuable product to offer.	____	____
2. **Physical comfort:** I have at hand all materials needed to make a sale. I ask my prospects to get what they'll need at hand before I begin.	____	____
3. **Pre-call planning:** I know what I'll say in each situation I'm likely to encounter. I know what information I'll need and where I can get it.	____	____
4. **Nervousness:** (If) I do not reveal any nervousness when talking to a prospect. My speech is clear and word choice understandable. My voice is under control.	____	____
5. **Voice:** I don't talk in a mon-		

otone, or too fast or too slow. Prospects hear and understand me.   ____   ____

6. **Selling strategy:** I always follow a system of basic selling steps. I prepare and deliver an orderly, easy-to-follow sales call.   ____   ____

7. **Enthusiasm:** I take a strong interest in my products. I work for a good company that is important to people.   ____   ____

8. **Attention-grabbers:** I use a strong opening remark to get the prospect's attention. I avoid jumping to conclusions that block my effectiveness.   ____   ____

9. **Sales message:** I am mentally prepared to respond to any situation when I pick up the telephone. In my selling, I stress what my product will do for the prospect.   ____   ____

10. **Listening:** I concentrate on the call I am handling, and avoid distractions. I don't interrupt my prospects.   ____   ____

11. **Empathy:** I react to the type of person I am talking with, tailoring my manner and message to the prospect's.   ____   ____

12. **Analysis:** I know what questions to ask to create listener interest, and learn the prospect's needs and wants. I get the whole story.   ____   ____

13. **Word use:** I have good enunciation and an extensive vocabulary. I use selling words. I evoke clear mental images and avoid using jargon.   ____   ____

14. **Action-getting presentations:** I sell the benefits of my product. I am enthusiastic. I stimulate a need or desire to buy.   ____   ____

15. **Flexibility:** I can put together an action-getting sales message that is tailored to a prospect's personality and needs. Quickly.   ____   ____

16. **Answering objections:** I react positively to objections, handling and disposing of one objection at a time. I employ a "price is value" strategy.   ____   ____

17. **Asking for the order:** I get the sales action I set out for. I am alert for buying signals and employ the trial close and other closing techniques.   ____   ____

18. **Controlling the interview:** I try to control the course and content of each call. I stick to my plan, and urge my prospects to do so when necessary.   ____   ____

19. **Paperwork:** My work is planned. I am well-organized. I keep my commitments and complete all necessary paperwork on time and according to instructions.   ____   ____

20. **Sales goals:** I have daily goals, and other periodic goal checkpoints. I regularly reach or exceed my quota.   ____   ____

21. **Customer service:** My attitude is to serve my customers and prospects in all of my dealings with them.   ____   ____

22. **Product knowledge:** I can distinguish among features, advantages, and benefits. I understand buying motives and the importance of selling benefits to meet them.   ____   ____

TOTALS   ____   ____

Now that you have completed the performance evaluation test you have a measure of your attitude toward and proficiency in the skills needed to succeed at teleselling. You should, from time to time (perhaps every three or six months), complete the questionnaire again. By comparing your score with the last one, you can evaluate your progress in strengthening your work on the telephone. Completing the test on a regular basis can also serve as a quick check to ensure that you are continuing to develop your skills in the right direction.

Afterword

Your completion of this book has gotten you off to a solid start in your teleselling career. If you already sell, but are now moving into teleselling, it no doubt brushed up your selling skills and made you aware of the differences between face-to-face and telephone selling. But remember, this is just your beginning. You have come far enough to now see other selling-skills books, especially those that urge numerous steps, keys, or secrets, in their proper light: as guides for possible behavior in situations that may (or may not) apply to your selling. Read them now, and any other magazines, newsletters, and publications that can help you in your work. Attend seminars. Study salespeople you know and admire. Talk with your peers. Telephone selling is an exciting field, one that is going to continue to grow and change in the future. It will be up to you to remain in command of effective new techniques and on top in your profession.

To encourage your professional reading and help you develop needed new skills, I have prepared a short bibliography. Most of the books listed should be available through your local bookstore or from the publisher. If any go out of print, you may be able to find them in a library.

Bibliography

Berman, John H. *Telephone Marketing Systems Manual of Operation*. Wellesley, Ma.: Danjon, 1983.

Bernstein, Theodore M. *Watch Your Language*. New York: Atheneum, 1958.

Brown, Michael T. *Making Money With the Telephone: The Complete Handbook of Telephone Marketing*. Ventura, Calif.: Future Shop, 1977.

Brownstone, David M. *Sell Your Way to Success*. New York: John Wiley & Sons, 1979.

Bury, Charles. *Telephone Techniques that Sell*. New York: Warner Books, 1980.

Flesch, Rudolf, and A. H. Lass. *A New Guide to Better Writing*. New York: Warner Books, 1982.

Goodman, Gary S. *Reach Out & Sell Someone*. Englewood Cliffs, N.J.: Prentice-Hall, 1983.

———. *Winning by Telephone*. Englewood Cliffs, N.J.: Prentice-Hall, 1982.

Hodges, John C., and Mary E. Whitten. *Harbrace College Handbook*, 9th edition. New York: Harcourt, Brace, Jovanovich, 1982.

Ling, Mona. *How to Increase Sales and Put Yourself Across by Telephone*. Englewood Cliffs, N.J.: Prentice-Hall, 1963.

Masser, Barry Z. and William M. Leeds. *Power Selling by Telephone*. Englewood Cliffs, N.J.: Prentice-Hall, 1982.

———. *Telephone Marketing and Territory Management*. Woodland Hills, Calif.: Intempo Communications, Inc., 1982.

Ortland, Gerald J. *Telemarketing*. New York: John Wiley & Sons, 1982.

Peterson, K. T. *How to Sell Successfully by Telephone*. Chicago: Dartnell Corp., 1975.

Pope, Jeffrey. *Business-to-Business Telemarketing*. New York: American Management Association, 1983.

Prevette, Earl. *How to Increase Your Sales by Telephone*. New York: C. & R. Anthony, 1963.

Reader's Digest. *Word Power*. New York: Berkley Publishing Corp., 1980.

Roman, Murray. *Telemarketing Campaigns That Work*. New York: McGraw-Hill Book Company, 1983.

———. *Telephone Marketing: How to Build Business by Telephone*. New York: McGraw-Hill Book Company, 1976.

Shafiroff, Martin D., and Robert L. Shook. *Successful Telephone Selling in the Eighties*. New York: Harper & Row, 1982.

Steckel, Robert C. *Profitable Telephone Sales Operations*. New York: Arco Publishing, 1976.

Appendix A

Call Flow Pattern

Your calls will follow a pattern as you progress from hello to asking for the order. The pattern that eventually emerges will be determined by a variety of factors, including your use of the 5-step system of selling, your call goal and strategy, and the behavior of your prospects. To better plan what you will say, as well as determine where best to plug in such things as preemptive statements, trial closes, and asking for the order, be aware of the call flow pattern that develops in your work on the telephone. To start, a sample is provided on the next page. It is an "ideal" call flow pattern growing from the 5-step call strategy.

For Thought and Action

How closely do your calls follow this "ideal" call flow pattern? What changes are necessary?

What would you say at each point represented by a block in the call flow pattern (or on your own call flow pattern where it differs)?

CALL FLOW PATTERN

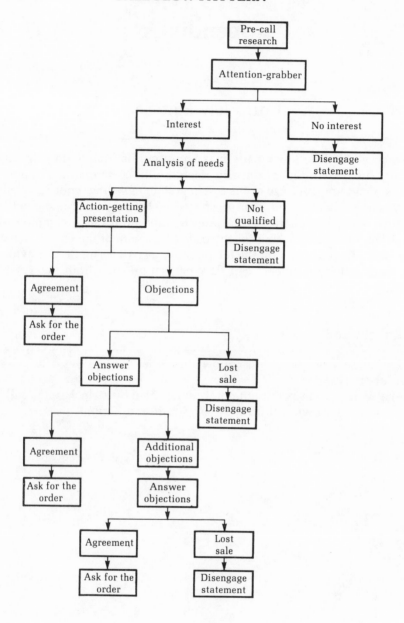

Appendix B

A Sample Multi-Call Work Plan

A major college-textbook publisher decided to implement a teleselling campaign to provide coverage to and increase sales at those schools which were not called on (because of size or sales volume) by an outside person. In colleges, individual instructors usually select their own textbooks. However, in certain basic courses (i.e., freshman composition, calculus, physics) it is not uncommon to have the decision made by a faculty committee. The approach adopted by the publisher illustrates both the power and reach of the telephone as a sales medium, and the benefit of integrating mail and telephone marketing into a complex, multi-contact selling situation.

After careful study, sales management and the telephone salespeople decided to limit coverage to 75 accounts (schools) during a cycle (see below) in a territory. The school year is divided into four complete selling cycles. The time spread of each cycle is tied to both the textbook-selection decision date (when orders have to be to the school's bookstore), and to the publication schedules of new books and revised editions of earlier books. The cycles, the products to be sold, and the marketing goals for each are as follows:

September–November: Sell new books published early (i.e., a 1986 book actually manufactured in the fall of 1985) and early new editions of previous books to professors using the previous edition.

November–January: Sell all books published (new, new editions, and existing) and available for shipment to all professors teaching second-semester-only courses. Sell supplements (study guides and books of readings/cases) to all professors using a related main volume during the second semester.

February–March: For the following school year, sell all new books to all professors teaching the appropriate course, and, where an appropriate existing title was published, all professors teaching large-enrollment courses.

April–May: Sell all books to professors or schools that have late book decision dates, and supplements to all professors in the territory who selected the related main volume.

With the above goals as guidelines, each teleseller is responsible for completing the following steps and calls in each selling cycle:

1. A sales letter is mailed to professors according to pre-call research which indicates that there might be a potential sale. The letter states the purpose of the contact—interest in new textbooks, textbook needs for other courses, or an announcement of the publication of a new edition of a book—and invites a request for further information.

2. Those responding with interest are sent a descriptive brochure and another sales letter inviting recipients to call or write for a free copy of the book to examine closely for possible selection. Note is made at this point of all professors teaching large-enrollment courses who did not request an examination copy of the relevant book.

3. Those requesting an examination copy of the book are sent one immediately, along with a brief cover letter.

4. One week after the examination copy is sent, a telephone call is placed to the professor. This straight sales call is intended to get the professor to look inside the book, to make him or her aware of the features/advantages/benefits the book has, and to ask for the order.

5. If the book is selected at this time, appropriate follow-up is scheduled. If other selling work is required before the selection can be finalized (more information, copies of supplements, availability of test banks, etc.) additional sales calls are planned. All calls to a professor are made in anticipation of asking for an order.

6. A final sales letter follows the "ask for the order" call, and depending on whether or not the order is placed, has different goals. If no order is received, a final letter stresses anew the benefits of the book in question (and perhaps now includes a list of those schools that have already selected the book), and asks that it be seriously reconsidered. To professors who selected the company's book, a thank-you letter, also promoting related supplements that can be ordered, is mailed and again followed by a telephone call to sell supplements.

7. If there is no response to step 1 above from professors teaching large-enrollment courses, the telephone is once more employed, this time as a follow-up to learn why there was no response. This step can lead to resuming the cycle with step 2, depending on what is learned.

Some items of related interest are worthy of note:

1. *Record keeping.* Each teleseller tracks his or her schools for each cycle. Tracking is based on potential dollar volume to be closed in that cycle. As a result, for a given cycle the list of the 75 schools being contacted could vary from previous cycles. The tellsellers are in ongoing contact with all major schools in their territory, perhaps as many as 100.

2. *Work volume.* Each teleseller produces approximately 3,500 letters per year. With three tellsellers, such a flow of correspondence makes word-

processing capability (an additional cost of teleselling) a must for the success of the operation.

3. *Teleseller identity*. Heavy emphasis is placed on the teleseller's establishing his or her name in the minds of the prospects and customers, just as a field representative would do. Their own business cards (with photograph), stationery, and note paper all let their contacts know who they are. It is estimated that the most successful of the tetesellers is known by as many as 300 instructors in her territory.

Appendix C

Developing a Script

You have been urged in this book to employ a planned but extemporaneous sales-call strategy whenever you can. Flexibility is a virtual requirement when you are teleselling to the business community and thus calling on knowledgeable or professional buyers. That consumer teleselling which involves either a sophisticated product or prospect can also require that you adapt your presentation to suit various prospects and situations.

There are, however, situations where a script may suit your needs or goals. Such activities as lead generation, trial offers, post-sale follow-up, replenishing or replacing supplies or parts; and such goals as qualifying leads, securing appointments, and one-call closes, can be quickly and easily handled by both veterans and new telesellers with a script. The following outline should help you create and deliver a scripted message.

Script Development

1. Attention-Grabber
   a. Introduction: your name and your company's name.
   b. Initial benefit statement: the reason for your call, including mention of your product by name, how it will benefit the prospect, and proof.
   Goal: to secure the attention and interest of the prospect and the time to present your product for consideration.
2. Analysis of Needs
   Asking questions: use closed questions to gather data, open questions for amplification or clarification.
   Goal: to learn prospect's problems and concerns and create needs and desires, all to help you select and present an appropriate product.
3. Action-Getting Presentation
   a. Renewal of interest: select a suitable presentation opener.
   b. Transition and body: make your product recommendation stressing benefits you know will satisfy needs and desires.
   c. Close: summarize and trial close.
   Goal: to present your product in terms that satisfy prospect needs and buying motivation.

4. Answering Objections
  a. Restating the objection: to be sure you understand it.
  b. Qualifying the objection: ask questions to analyze the causes of the objection.
  c. Answering the objection: stress benefits.
  d. Close: secure agreement with your response.
  Goal: to remove the obstacles to getting the sales action you want.
5. Asking for the Order
  Closing techniques: use an appropriate technique to secure agreement.
  Goal: to achieve your call objective as a natural conclusion to the call.
6. Wrapping Up and Hanging Up
  Disengage: a statement or closing to conclude the call without further conversation.
  Goal: to get off the telephone before the prospect has time to reconsider.

Sample Script I

The following script was developed by a consulting firm for use by tele-sellers in securing appointments for its outside salespeople.

Hello, Mr. Wallace. I'm Steve Johnson with MMS, Inc. We specialize in management development systems tailored to the food-processing industry. Such clients as Kellogg's, French's and Hanover Brands have documented increases in productivity as high as 40 percent using our techniques. I'm calling to share some of those techniques with you.

To better determine which of our materials can serve you, I'll need answers to a few brief questions. How many employees does your plant have? (pause) How many supervisors do you employ? (pause) Then each supervisor manages the work of _____ employees, is that right Mr. Wallace?

Do you presently make use of the employee participation concept, such as Quality Circles, in company decision-making, Mr. Wallace? (pause)
(IF "YES")

How has that worked for you? (IF NO DISSATISFACTION, DISENGAGE AND HANG UP)
(IF "NO")

Have you ever considered using such programs?
(IF "YES")

Which ones? (pause) Those are excellent programs. Given their wide acceptance and good results, why were they not implemented?
(IF "NO")

Mr. Wallace, the MMS Team Builder program has shown, in numerous companies in your industry, it can reduce absenteeism and turnover, increase productivity, moderate labor tension, and improve morale. Which of these problems are your greatest concern? (pause) Are there any other factors at work

*in your company that you feel are also limiting your workers' ability to pro-
duce to their maximum potential? (pause) Would you elaborate on why?
(pause)*

*Mr. Wallace, you are right to include management attitude as one of the
barriers to implementing an employee participation program and improving
your plant's productivity as a result. MMS Team Building starts with management. Our service includes two full days of orientation to insure that top
management at your firm has a realistic, positive attitude and expectation of
the program. And we follow up with intermittent reports to top management
on the progress we are making with your people. Would you agree that this
initial step and our follow-up will solve the management attitude problem for
you? (pause)*
(IF "YES," CONTINUE)
(IF "NO," ASK "WHY" AND ADDRESS)

*Another benefit of the MMS Team Builder concept, growing out of our
unique "Team Form" procedure, deals with your concern about an immediate positive impact on morale. This in turn reduces absenteeism and labor/
management tension, and, in the long run, turnover. Are those your most
pressing concerns? (pause) Trained MMS personnel conduct initial sessions
with all affected employees to solicit participation. These same MMS staff
members then train your team builders and conduct the first team meeting.
You benefit in three ways:*

*First, you can begin reaping the benefits of employee participation on day
one, while preparing to eventually take over the full program at your own pace.*

*Second, your people are trained on-the-job, not in a classroom. They not
only gain invaluable hands-on experience, but learn to deal with their own
work and problems, not hypothetical situations. And, the workability of the
program is demonstrated to those who are key to its success, the workers
themselves.*

*Third, you save money. All our development programs take place on-site.
You do not have the expense of sending people to seminars in faraway cities,
and lose valued employees for perhaps weeks.*

*Aren't these among the benefits you sought when you looked at other
employee participation programs, Mr. Wallace? (pause)*
(IF "NO") *What else were you looking for? (pause)*
(CLOSE AND GO ON)
(IF "YES")

*Mr. Wallace, I will have a representative in Philadelphia next week. I
would like her to sit down with you and share our employee participation
techniques and program with you. What day would be most convenient for
you? (pause)*
(IF "YES," SECURE APPOINTMENT AND DISENGAGE)
(IF "WHY DON'T YOU SEND ME SOME LITERATURE ON 'TEAM BUILD-
ERS'? I'LL LOOK IT OVER AND GET BACK TO YOU.")

*The brochures covering all aspects of this program total 46. Mr. Wallace,
I know you are a busy man. Do you have time to read though 46 detailed brochures by next week? (pause) And one key benefit of the MMS Team Builder*

is its adaptability to each client situation. When you have installed the program, it will be unlike any of the more than 120 others we have in place. Wouldn't you find it easier to spend 20 minutes with our representative? (pause)
(IF "YES," SET APPOINTMENT AND DISENGAGE)

Thank you for your time, Mr. Wallace. Ms. Kelly will see you next week. If others in your company should attend, invite as many as 10 people, those you think may be involved in the decision. We look forward to your reaction to our unique concept.

Sample Script II

This script was developed by a firm that publishes financial planning materials for individuals described as "well-to-do." It is intended to secure orders for a new publication, and employs the "offer close."

Hello, Mrs. Curtis, I'm Fran Bailey with Hester and Ernst, financial publishers. I'm calling you because your subscription to our Financial Planning Report leads me to believe you would benefit from our new Budgeting and Financial Independence Manual.

Our new manual shows you how to plan for and control every type of personal financial need. With nearly 300 user-tested forms, reports, sample spread sheets, charts and analyses for your use, Budgeting and Financial Independence Manual can help you plan and monitor cash flow, asset growth, and investment returns, whether your financial planning system is manual or computer maintained.

The reason for my call now is that the Budgeting and Financial Independence Manual is ready for your examination on a 30-day approval basis. I'd like to send you a copy to look over on that basis so you can use it and see that it suits your needs.
(IF "YES," CONFIRMS ADDRESS AND DISENGAGE)
(IF "NO")

Mrs. Curtis, you'll be pleased to know that the Manual comes in its own box, suitable for return shipment. And, we include a check for $2.50 to cover return postage. Should you decide the Manual is not everything you expect or want, there is no cost, obligation, or inconvenience to you. Won't you okay delivery of this new publication and see for yourself how useful it can be to your effort to reach financial independence?
(IF "YES," CONFIRM ADDRESS AND DISENGAGE)
(IF "NO," DISENGAGE)

Index